the simple guide to SHOWING Your Dog

t.f.h.

T.F.H. Publications, Inc.

Richard G. Beauchamp

Contents

Part One: The Cast of Characters **11**

Chapter 1... What is a Dog Show? 13

Where Dog Showing Took Me 15

First Things First 16

The American Kennel Club 18

United Kennel Club 18

American Rare Breed Association 19

States Kennel Club 19

The Kennel Club 19

Conformation Shows 20

Match Shows 21

Championship Shows 23

Invitational Shows 23

The Cast of Characters 24

Are Dog Shows Good for Dogs? 29

Going for the Gold 31

Words from the Wise 33

Chapter 2....The Breeds, The Groups, and Their Purposes 35

Making the Right Choice .36

The Sporting Group 38

The Hound Group 38

The Working Group 41

The Terrier Group 42

The Toy Group 44

The Non-Sporting Group .45

The Herding Group 46

The Miscellaneous Group 46

Selecting the Right Breed 47

The Fabled "Great One" 48

Chapter 3 ...What Makes a Great Show Dog? 51

The Breed Standard 55

Finding a Show Dog 66

Breeding Your Own Winner 66

What to Expect 74

Chapter 4....Getting Your Dog Ready for the Ring 75

Peddling to the Top 78

Anatomy 101 82

Health Watch 88

A Word on Nutrition 93

Grooming 96

Words from the Wise 100

Chapter 5....Socializing and Training Your Show Dog 103

Lessons to Learn 105

Training 111

Crate Training 111

Table Manners 115

Free Stacking and Baiting 121

Practice Makes Perfect 124

Words from the Wise .126

How to Stack Your Dog Page 121

Chapter 6....Traveling with Your Dog 129

Auto Travel 129

Time and Temperature .130

Safety First 131

Identification and Medication 132

Packing Your Dog's Suitcase 133

Rooms at the Inn 135

Traveling by Air 136

Part Two: Show Business . . . .

Chapter 7... It's Show Time! 143

The All-Breed Dog Show 143

The Specialty Show 147

Non-Regular Dog Show Classes 148

Premium Lists 151

Dog Show Classes 155

The Ring Patterns Page 163-166

Judging Schedules 157

When You Arrive 159

Problems and Solutions 160

Ring Procedures 161

Keeping Perspective 166

Words from the Wise 167

Chapter 8...The Big Time 171

The Dog of Great Type 172

Shooting for the Stars .178

The Ratings System 178

Paths to the Top 182

Words from the Wise 187

Chapter 9...Other Shows and Events 189

Obedience 190

Canine Good Citizen test 191

Agility 193

Herding Tests and Trials 194

Tracking 197

Field Trials 197

Flyball 200

Rally-O 201

Therapy Work 202

Words from the Wise 203

Glossary 205

Resources 211

Index 217

Foreword

"I'm bored–there's nothing to do!" It's the cry of the restless teenager. I can remember having said the same thing myself–often. That is, until I discovered the wonderful world of dogs.

My life took an abrupt turn the day I walked through the fairgrounds turnstile to my first dog show. I can honestly say from that day on through to today as I look over the completed chapters of this book, there has never been a day of my life that I could say, "There's nothing to do." Usually my complaint and dilemma is that there is never quite enough time to give attention to the continually expanding horizon the dog game provides.

Purebred dogs as an activity seems to have a siren call all its own, and there's hardly an animal lover alive that can resist it. Nor is there a talent known to mankind that somehow can't find an adaptation applicable to the challenge of purebred dogs–particularly in the show ring. The athlete's dexterity and endurance, the dancer's sense of rhythm and flair, the artist's ability to create beauty from raw material–all these and more apply, to say nothing of what an ideal home showing dogs provides for the competitive spirit.

Much has been written of how to prepare a given breed's coat for the ring and a good deal more on performance. Little, however, has been said about the thought processes that bring focus to all the talents and abilities that prepare a person for those fleeting but critical few minutes in the ring. I've known the best of dogdom's owner-handlers and have had at least a modicum of success at showing my own dogs. What all of us have experienced is part and parcel of what appears on the following pages.

When reading this, pay particular attention to the Words from the Wise. They contain advise from the greatest source possible–those who have tried and succeeded. Hopefully what we have learned along the way will prove beneficial to you in your journey to the top.

Part One

The Cast of Characters

"It's okay, kid. You lost your first dog show, sure, but at least you resisted the primal instinct to beg."

What Is a Dog Show?

Dog shows and dog breeding have long attracted the interest of people ranging from royalty to the lady next door. The backgrounds of dog fanciers are as varied as you could possibly imagine. As a dog breeder and judge, I've known ordinary family folk who have attended shows and competed successfully with top-notch dogs they've bred themselves. Their dogs stand right along side those owned by people with unlimited financial means. Good dog show judges disregard all but the dogs themselves when making the final decision. Who you are and where you come from doesn't matter in good judging—it's the dogs that have to prove themselves, not the people.

People from varied backgrounds participate in dog showing.

Dog show people all share an appreciation of a dog's great qualities.

The fact that you've picked up this book and are reading it says that you have the prerequisite for being involved in what we dog show die-hards lovingly call "the dog game." It's not anything magical or unique; it's quite simply a love of dogs.

With few exceptions, the people you'll meet at a dog show share an appreciation for their dogs' devotion and willingness to accept humans exactly as they are. It's hard to find that kind of fidelity in many places outside the canine world.

During your journey through the world of dog showing, you might hear all kinds of tales about showing purebred dogs, told by those who are usually on the outside looking in. You might hear naysayers criticizing the sport: "It's a cult." "They're all madly obsessive." "Their dogs are spoiled rotten!" You'll definitely hear about the politics, the enormous amounts of money people spend on the dogs, how much the dogs hate it–the list goes on and on.

That's Show Biz!

Those of you who have seen the mocumentary *Best In Show,* by Christopher Guest, might wonder if only odd-balls are allowed to enter the world of dog showing. To tell the truth, the film does depict some of our particular human oddities. However, realize that there wouldn't have been much fun or interest in portraying the ordinary guy or gal involved in dog showing, nor would a movie about purebred dogs as a family activity be box office boffo. Hollywood's portrayal of dog shows is a reflection of Hollywood itself—far bigger and far more colorful than life can ever hope to be. Tinsel Town paints in very broad strokes!

Speaking as someone who's spent an entire lifetime involved with purebred dogs, I'm the first to admit that we do have our unforgettable characters, as does just about any hobby or profession. Actually, rank-and-file dog people are rather ordinary and down-to-earth folk who simply have a deep appreciation for the canine world's many good qualities.

It's from there–from our acknowledgement of our dogs' many positive attributes–that people in the dog game begin. Where the game takes you depends wholly upon your individual interests in the sport. Breeding, exhibiting, judging, training, and teaching–you'll find a place to do it all.

Where Dog Showing Took Me

I walked into my first dog show in Detroit, Michigan, a lifetime ago, when I was still in elementary school, and somehow I've never left. I was away briefly for college, and then while I took a job with *Daily Variety,* but it's as if those times were mere blips when I review my life in dogs. The dog game is really an addiction of sorts, and it hooked me early.

One of the things that keeps us all involved is the fact that the dog game is ever changing. Personally speaking, I find it difficult to remain enthusiastic and involved with something that drones on forever and never seems to grow, develop, or change. But if you enjoy participating in a game that is continually evolving, then this is definitely the place for you.

Interest in dog showing often begins with a deep love of dogs.

That said, the dog game is a place where you have a friend, and nine times out of ten, a place to stay, no matter where in the world you might travel. Dog folk are "family," regardless of the breed they favor or where they live. My own experience stands in testament to that.

The two years I was in the military were all spent at Camp Chaffe, Arkansas, a desolate outpost located about a half-hour away from the small town of Ft. Smith, which is near absolutely nothing, or so it seemed to this big-city-born youngster.

I was looking through the yellow pages of the Ft. Smith telephone directory shortly after my arrival and came across a small advertisement placed there for an Afghan Hound kennel. I had a weekend pass and no place to go, so I called the owners of the kennel and told them I had been involved with dogs back in Michigan.

The author awarding a ribbon to Ch. Dwynella April Love, owned by Dede Rodgers.

In order to get into dog showing, you need a purebred dog.

They invited me to their home and, in an evening, we established a friendship that would last many years. The owners of the kennel opened their home to me, and I practically lived there for the remainder of my military stint. I traveled to shows with them, learned a great deal about how to care for their breed, and was even given the opportunity to handle their outstanding dogs at the shows we attended.

I've also found that the same spirit of camaraderie extends itself to the four corners of the world. Whether it was Hong Kong or Cape Town, Florence or Sydney, I have never been further than a telephone call away from a welcoming friend. It's always wonderful, if not a bit crazy and hectic at times, but if you are able to keep your priorities straight, you'll have the best time of your life.

First Things First

There's just one prerequisite for the dog show game–you'll need a dog–a purebred dog, of course, and the better the quality of that dog, the more fun you're apt to have. All of which takes us right back to where we started, with you picking up this book. Obviously, you have an interest in dogs, and it appears you just might be thinking about showing one. So let's take a look at what goes on and how you might join in the fun.

The first recorded formally organized dog show was held in Newcastle-upon-Tyne, England in June of 1859. Because of Great Britain's reputation for excellence in animal husbandry, it's probably not suprising that dog showing began in England. Countless breeds of cattle, sheep, and horses trace their origins to British ingenuity, and a quick overview of our many breeds of dogs reveals an overwhelming majority with British origins or development.

The Newcastle show was limited to Setters and Pointers, but, within a few years, shows for multiple breeds were being held. As breeds were added to these events, more and more people were attracted and became involved. By 1873 it became obvious that organization and record keeping were necessary. The establishment of The Kennel Club, the first purebred dog registry ever organized, accomplished this.

Originally dog shows were organized as a place where breeders could show off their stock.

Dog shows were originally organized as a place for breeders to gather to have their breeding stock evaluated by someone experienced and knowledgeable in their respective breed. The person given that responsibility made his or her selections based upon the theory that superior dogs were the most likely to contribute their good qualities to succeeding generations. The judge arrived at those decisions by comparing the dogs in the ring to a written description of an ideal specimen of the breed. Those descriptions are known as the breed standards. All of the characteristics that collectively define the ideal specimen of the breed are listed in the standard. Of the dogs appearing before the judge, the one that possessed most of those characteristics described in the standard was put into first place. The dog coming

What Is a Breed Standard?

A breed standard is a detailed description of an individual breed. It is meant to portray the ideal specimen of that breed. The description includes ideal structure, coat, temperament, and gait—all aspects of the dog. Because the standard describes an ideal specimen, it isn't based on any particular dog. It is a concept against which judges compare actual dogs, and breeders strive to produce dogs that adhere to this standard. At a dog show, the dog that wins is the one that comes closest, in the judge's opinion, to the standard for its breed. Breed standards are written by the breed parent clubs—the national organizations formed to oversee the well-being of the breed. The standards are voted on and approved by the members of the parent clubs

Most dog shows in the US are governed by the American Kennel Club.

The Stud Book

The American Kennel Club maintains The Stud Book, which is a record of every dog ever registered with the organization, and publishes a variety of materials on purebred dogs, including a monthly magazine, books, and numerous educational pamphlets. For more information, contact the AKC at the address listed in Resources at the end of this book.

closest in quality to the first-place dog was placed second, and so on down the line. This process continues to this day.

The American Kennel Club

If you live in the United States and are planning to show dogs, you'll most likely be showing your dogs under the auspices of the American Kennel Club, usually referred to simply as the AKC. The organization maintains offices in both New York City and Raleigh, North Carolina.

The AKC is a nonprofit organization devoted to the advancement of purebred dogs. It maintains a registry of recognized breeds and adopts and enforces rules for dog events, including shows, obedience trials, field trials, hunting tests, lure coursing, herding, earthdog trials, agility, and the Canine Good Citizen program.

The AKC, established in 1884, refers to itself as "a club of clubs," and today is composed of more than 500 independent dog clubs throughout the United States. A delegate represents each club. The delegates make up the legislative body of the AKC, voting on rules and electing directors.

The AKC is the largest purebred dog registry in the United States, but other domestic registries also exist. Each of these registry sources has its own system of registration and area of specialization. Their addresses and contact information can be found in Resources at the end of this book.

United Kennel Club

Heading the list of alternative domestic registries is the United Kennel Club (UKC), headquartered in Kalamazoo, Michigan. The UKC is the second-oldest and second-largest, all-breed dog registration. The UKC strongly supports the "Total Dog" concept, meaning that the ideal dog is one who not only looks as its breed standard requires but also is able to perform in the manner for which the breed was developed. Single breed and multi-breed shows are sponsored by the UKC throughout the United States. The organization registers all-breeds but has historically focused on the many Coonhound breeds developed in North America. As a result, the UKC legitimately claims the largest Coonhound registry in the world.

American Rare Breed Association (ARBA)

As its name implies, the ARBA specializes in the less-common breeds. Breeds developed in foreign countries are judged by the standard used in their country of origin. The ARBA decides which standard should be used for breeds developed in the United States. The organization holds all-breed dog shows throughout the country.

States Kennel Club (SKC)

The youngest US kennel club, it was founded in the mid-1980s and organized to give exhibitors one more choice in respect to registries and shows in which to exhibit. The organization recognizes all other registries.

The Kennel Club

Because England was the first country to organize a registry source for purebred dogs in 1873, their official designation, *The* Kennel Club, was all that was necessary at the time and remains so as far as the British are concerned. However, most American

UKC Red Bone Coonhound, Grand Ch. "PR" Wabash River Shadow, owned and handled by Curtis Elburn.

Although the AKC is the largest registry, other domestic clubs also hold dog shows.

The Kennel Club in England was the first to register purebred dogs.

exhibitors refer to the organization as "England's Kennel Club," or "The Kennel Club in England." Today, The Kennel Club in England is still one of the most famous and respected dog breeding registries in the world.

Conformation Shows

Dog show events run the gamut from the more formal events that you see broadcast frequently on television to the exciting agility and herding trials and the slightly more formal (but incredibly useful) Canine Good Citizen events. We'll take a closer look at all the different events you will be able to participate later in this book.

The biggest and most well-attended events are called conformation shows. This is where dogs are awarded points based on how closely they compare to the written standard of their breed. There are a number of different kinds of conformation events, ranging from informal puppy matches to championship and invitational shows.

Conformation shows were originally organized by breeders who wanted to know how the dogs they were breeding stacked up to the standard, as well as how their dogs compared to the dogs that their neighboring breeders were producing. Today, however, not everyone who enjoys showing dogs intends to become a breeder. Many exhibitors find enjoyment simply in the competitive aspect of these events.

Conformation dog shows are open to all non-neutered and non-spayed purebred dogs registered with the American Kennel Club or the organization sponsoring the event. Conformation events of some

Conformation shows are the largest and most well-attended events in the dog world.

kind are held every weekend of the year in one part of the country or another, with the exception of the last two weeks of December.

That year-end break is theoretically set aside to allow exhibitors to observe the holidays. However, you're more apt to find the die-hards plotting and getting ready for the following year's campaign, which will resume immediately after the beginning of the new year.

Generally speaking, conformation shows fall into two major categories: matches and championship events. Match shows are primarily staged for the young or inexperienced dogs that are not quite ready to compete for championship points. In most cases, classes are offered for dogs from about three months of age and older.

Match Shows

Match shows are a great place for beginners, both human and canine, to learn what dog shows are all about. That said, even a lot of experienced owners like to take their puppies and young dogs to matches for training and to get them a little ring-wise before moving on to championship events.

Matches are far more informal than championship events. They are more laid-back, and there's plenty of time for the novice handler to make mistakes along with everyone else. It's the place where you can ask questions and seek assistance from more experienced exhibitors or from the officiating judges of the day.

These competitive events take place almost everywhere throughout the country. Major cities have large membership clubs that put on dog shows with two and three thousand dogs, but there are many well-organized, smaller kennel clubs as well. The entries at these shows are usually under a thousand dogs, but the quality of the competition often runs just as high as one might find in the larger entry shows.

Match shows are great places to get your puppy used to the show ring.

All-Breed Matches

All-breed matches are open to all breeds eligible for registration with the AKC. These all-breed matches progress toward the day's finale (called Best in Match) the same way championship shows move toward Best in Show.

It's really very helpful for beginners to start showing at this level, because matches allow them to learn ring procedure and where they need to be at certain times. Mistakes are very common at matches, and no one thinks poorly of those making them. Everyone there realizes that part of the purpose of these events is to learn how to do things the right way.

Specialty Matches

Specialty matches are conducted in the same informal way as the all-breed matches, but they are sponsored by clubs devoted to one particular breed and are open only to dogs of that breed. When there is a club devoted to a specific breed in an area, that club will often hold these match shows so that the newer club members and young puppies will have an opportunity to gain some experience.

Specialty matches are only open to a particular breed of dog.

Breeders are usually aware of local matches for their own breed, and, if you have any interest, you can usually check with your dog's breeder as to when and where these matches are held. Information regarding specialty matches can also be found in the classified sections of Sunday newspapers under "Dogs for Sale" or "Pets" listings.

A good thing about all-breed or specialty matches is that you can almost always enter your dog in them on the day of the show. Most clubs accept entries on the grounds of the show site on the morning of the event. The person taking your entry will be able to help you fill out the form and give you the preliminary instructions you will need.

Normally, the only information you need to enter a match is listed on your puppy's registration certificate. It's a good idea to make a photocopy of your puppy's or dog's registration to take along with you. That way you'll have all the information you need but won't run the risk of losing that important document.

Championship Shows

Championship shows reflect everything you learned at the match level but on a more formal and tightly organized basis. This is where you can win points counting toward a championship.

I strongly suggest you consider entering championship shows only after you've had a bit of experience showing at matches and attending handling classes. We'll take a look at some of the ways you can prepare yourself for the championship show in later chapters.

Great Dane Ch. Harley D's Eat Your Hardt Out, TD, owned and handled by Joanne Blair, wins Best of Breed.

Championship shows have fairly rigid time schedules, and most of the people there have had at least some dog show experience. A person who has never competed at a show on this level is bound to feel somewhat bewildered. Everyone seems "expert" by comparison and is rushing to stay on schedule.

Championship shows are sponsored by various all-breed kennel clubs, or in some instances, by a club specializing in one particular breed of dog. In these specialty shows, entries are limited to that single breed alone.

Join the Club

The AKC can provide you with the name of the all-breed kennel club in your area and will also know if there is a local club devoted to your particular breed. Once you are in touch with these clubs and have become a member, you will know well in advance the dates of any future championship events.

Invitational Shows

There are a few special "invitational" events held throughout the year. These are restricted to dogs that have achieved certain qualifying levels. Some of these shows require that the

As You advance in dog showing, the competition becomes more elite.

A good breeder will be able to recognize the show prospects in a litter.

dogs have won Best in Show. Other invitational events invite dogs that have won sufficiently in the course of the year and those included among the top winners in their respective breeds.

When you're first getting started, you probably won't have to concern yourself with these "big gun" competitions. That said, it's often surprising how quickly some exhibitors progress from rank novice to one of the top winners in their breed.

The Cast of Characters

There are interests and talents that have gone into developing the various divisions that comprise today's dog game. Let's take a look at whom you might expect to meet at just about any dog show.

The Breeder

Some people are blessed with what I like to refer to as a sense of "stockmanship," an interest and ability to breed quality animals. Worldwide urbanization has put severe limitations on those who have a desire to express this ability in cattle or horses, but dog shows provide them with an outlet that would be otherwise unavailable.

Dog shows are the place where they're able to show off their accomplishments in breeding good stock. The breeder is the backbone of the purebred dog phenomenon.

It is important for beginners to align themselves with successful breeders, because long-time experience has given these people a unique and deep understanding of the essence of their respective breeds. They know the characteristics that separate good dogs from those that are purely mediocre, and they know what makes a great dog stand out above the rest.

Finding the Right Breeder

Respected breeders always have time for the beginner because they know their breed's future relies upon sincere and dedicated new people taking up the breed's cause. However, successful breeders are busy people. You'll seldom find them standing around with nothing to do at dog shows. More often than not, they're apt to be getting their dogs ready for the ring, showing the dogs, or attending to the dogs that have already been shown.

Respected breeders strive to produce the best dogs possible.

Top Ten Questions to Ask a Breeder

The number of dogs a breeder has in his or her breeding program has little to do with the quality of the dogs produced. Today, many outstanding breeding programs are conducted on a limited basis in the homes of breeders. Others are conducted on a larger scale with actual kennel facilities. The importance is not in how many but in how good; whether the dogs are large or small, raised in home or large kennel, these are facts that should be determined if you are looking for a dog to show.

1. Is the breeder a member of the national and/or local breed club?

2. How many champions has the breeder actually bred?

3. How long has the breeder been involved with the breed?

4. Does the breeder follow all breed-club recommendations for hereditary defect testing of the dogs used in the breeding program?

5. Will the breeder sell you, the beginner, a dog that is good enough to win?

6. Has the breeder assisted beginners in the past?

7. Will you be able to come to the breeder for advice and assistance once you have begun to show?

8. If the dog proves not to be a winner, is there compensation or the possibility of replacement?

9. Under what conditions would the breeder consider replacing a dog?

10. Does the breeder think that you would be a good candidate to learn how to show his or her breed?

Responsible breeders will only breed the healthiest dogs in order to carry on their best qualities.

The judge has the experience and knowledge to choose the dog that is closest to the standard.

Purchase or borrow books and magazines that are devoted to the breed in which you are interested. See which kennels are breeding the frequent winners and producers. When you attend shows, pay attention to the dogs that are most often in the winner's circle. Purchase a show catalogue that lists all the dogs entered in that show and check to see who bred the winning dogs. Sometimes the breeder and the owner are the same person, but the person that you want to get in touch with is the breeder of the dogs you see winning frequently.

Because most breeders are busy at a show, wait for a convenient moment and ask if there will be time in the course of the day to talk about your interest in the breed. If not, ask for their business card or make an appointment to visit their kennel and see their dogs.

Without a doubt, the successful breeder represents the beginner's fountain of knowledge. There are many questions the novice will ask of a breeder along the way, but the first one that should always be asked is "how should I begin?"

The Judge
In the early days of dog shows, the experienced and successful individuals within the breeders' ranks were called upon to decide which of the dogs entered in the competitions were worthy of acknowledgement and potentially useful as breeding stock. As shows increased in number, the need for more and more of these decision-makers grew and the highly specialized judges' profession developed.

Part 1

Ring Stewards

Judging takes place according to a time schedule. It is extremely important that the judge adheres to his or her schedule in order to accommodate the flow of events leading to the day's finals. Some of the judging details–paperwork and such–are handled at the ring, but the judge does not necessarily attend to them personally. To assist the judge in staying on schedule, clubs that host the show provide assistants known as ring stewards.

These individuals are experienced in ring procedure, and although they have no involvement in the judges' decisions, they assist in giving out armbands (which identify contestants) and occasionally serve as intermediaries between exhibitor and judge. Judges themselves know how important an experienced and efficient ring steward is to the competition's progress.

The ring steward helps to keep the show on schedule and assists the judge in the ring.

Ring stewards nearly always wear an identifying badge on their lapel or dress, and, in the rare case that they do not, the ring steward stands along side of the table holding the ribbons and trophies. He or she distributes armbands and will often pass along the judges' instructions as to where exhibitors should place their dog when they enter the ring.

Ring stewards can answer most questions an exhibitor might have in regard to ring procedure. Because they act as intermediaries for the judge, they are the appropriate people to go through if the exhibitor has a question he or she would like to ask the judge.

The Breeder-Exhibitor

Even in the earliest days of dog shows, it quickly became apparent to breeders that good hygiene, artful grooming, and the dexterity to present one's dogs in the ring beneficially enhanced the look of the dog and increased chances of winning. Some breeders mastered these techniques well, and, in addition to their breeding achievements, gained respect for their in-ring accomplishments. They became what we now call our breeder-exhibitors.

A professional handler shows dogs for other people.

They not only breed outstanding dogs, but are also able to present them advantageously as well, about which we will learn later in the book.

The Professional Handler

Needless to say, not all breeders are blessed with the same abilities when it comes to the presentation of a good dog. Those who lack the physical or artistic ability required to adequately present their dogs turn to people who have mastered the arts of grooming, conditioning, and presenting. Many of the dogs shown today journey to shows with professional handlers employed to condition and show them.

Simply put, a professional handler is an individual who shows dogs for those who cannot or choose not to show their own dog. He or she charges a fee for providing this service, which can be limited to meeting the owner at ringside and showing the dog. However, it can extend far beyond just that. The services of many of these professionals include ring training, conditioning, and grooming.

Usually when a professional is employed to show a dog to its championship, the handler will keep the dog at his or her kennel facility so that conditioning and training can be closely monitored. The dog will then travel to the shows as part the handler's "string."

Professional handlers once began as amateurs themselves, probably showing their own dogs. Their handling ability, professional attitude, and success in the ring led others to seek out their services. Usually beginning on a part-time basis, the best of these individuals often become so successful that handling becomes their sole livelihood.

The Amateur Handler

By far, the largest segment of the dog-exhibiting population is made up of people who, like yourself, simply love to show their own dogs. They have no particular desire to breed dogs or to show dogs for other people, but they find great enjoyment in their accomplishments with their own dogs. They love the challenge and competition showing dogs provides. These may be referred to as "amateur" handlers, but often their expertise has permitted them to compete successfully with the best of the professionals and achieve outstanding show records. There are many cases in which amateurs in a breed have become so skilled that they provide greater competition than the very best professional does.

The Dog Show Superintendent

The dog show superintendent is the person who understands the show process and has the organizational skills to run a dog show and attend to all of its tiny details. Dog show superintendents are approved and authorized by the AKC and operate independently. They oversee and administrate every facet of a dog show, from notifying potential exhibitors of coming events to providing entry forms for the events and arranging time schedules based upon the number of dogs entered.

You can understand how important scheduling is for championship shows when as many as 3,000 or 4,000 dogs are judged on a given day. However, what may appear as mass confusion to the novice is really a carefully orchestrated series of events.

Are Dog Shows Good for Dogs?

So far, all of this has been about the dog *people*. What about the dogs themselves? What do they think about all this? Are the dogs willing participants or, as some

An amateur handler is someone who enjoys showing his or her own dogs.

Many people are involved with running a successful dog show.

Part 1

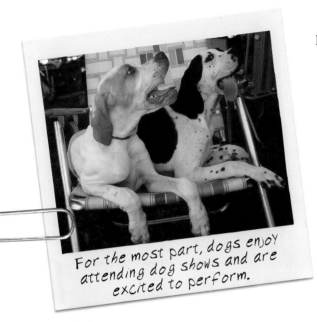

For the most part, dogs enjoy attending dog shows and are excited to perform.

Show dogs are happiest when with their owners.

people claim, are they being forced to participate in something that's more cruel than fun?

In my experience, dogs thoroughly enjoy the attention and companionship involved in showing, and they only suffer when they cannot be a part of the fun. As proof of what I'm going say on this subject, I would gladly invite anyone to join me (or anyone else who shows dogs) on a morning when dogs are being loaded into the car or van to drive off to a dog show.

Just try and leave behind one of the dogs accustomed to being shown. If you want to hear what cruel and unusual punishment sounds like, you need only listen to one of the dogs left behind. We can never leave the tailgate or door open to our vehicle while a stay-at-home dog is loose on the premises, because it's nearly impossible to coax the determined fellow to come out and stay behind.

Another example of our dogs' love of shows is seen when an exhibitor decides to show a retired dog in the Veterans Class at a special show. This is usually a former champion who earned an outstanding record as a youngster but hasn't been to a show in years. The joy and excitement exhibited by these old-timers when they're back in the ring is enough to bring a tear to the eye of even the most jaded member of the audience.

Common sense tells you that a dog likes to be with its master. How many dogs are given the opportunity to spend all week long at home with their master as well as every waking (and often sleeping!) moment of their weekend with their "adored ones" as well? How many dogs are constantly brushed, petted, and pampered and given the opportunity to visit all their canine pals the way dogs are at dog shows?

Quite frankly, every show dog I've ever owned wouldn't trade being the center of attention day in and day out for the world. If they hated it as much as some would have you believe, why in the world would they stand on each other's backs in order to be the next one chosen to be put up on the grooming table or taken into the ring? These are just a few examples of why I feel dog showing is such a positive experience for the dogs who participate.

The time spent with your dog training and competing helps to build a special bond.

Going for the Gold

In order for a dog registered with the AKC to become a champion, the dog must be awarded a total of 15 championship points. These points are awarded at licensed championship events to the best male and best female non-champions in each breed. The number of championship points that can be won at a particular show is based on the number of entries in a dog's own breed and sex entered at the show. Of the 15 points required, 2 of the wins must be what are called "majors" (i.e., 3 or more points). These two majors have to be won under two different judges.

Catalogs sold at all championship shows list the particulars relevant to every dog entered in the show, such as the dog's registered name, owner and breeder, and the dog's sire and dam. The catalog also lists the number of dogs required in each breed to win, from one through five points.

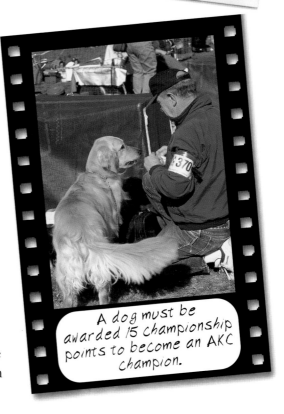

A dog must be awarded 15 championship points to become an AKC champion.

For the "Last Word" On Dog Shows

The American Kennel Club is the ultimate authority on all matters relating to dog shows and registration. Anyone interested in showing a dog is strongly advised to obtain a copy of the booklet, *Rules Applying to Registration and Dog Shows,* published by the AKC. This informative booklet is available free of charge and includes information regarding all aspects of registering and showing purebred dogs.

The number of dogs necessary for the various numbers of points differs geographically. For instance, it might take 25 Rottweiler males to win a 3-point major in California but only 16 in Michigan. These numbers are devised by the AKC and are based upon the average number of dogs shown in that breed's sex within a given area in a 12-month period. The numbers and their corresponding points are revised each year to reflect the level of competition in the previous year.

Don't worry if you don't understand all of this right now. As you go along, asking questions at shows and competing with your own dogs, you'll come to understand the point system, especially if your dog wins!

Now that you've gotten some dog show lingo under your collar and have a basic understanding of what a dog show is about, let's take a look at the most important part of dog showing–the dog.

Words from the Wise

Wingate Mackay-Smith
Bull Terriers

Sure, the idea is to win points, but having your dog judged fairly in your class is important as well. Mrs. Wingate Mackay-Smith–"Winkie" to her friends–and I met more years ago than either of us would wish to count. She was showing a Colored Bull Terrier whose name was "Benson" (officially Ch. Banbury Benson of Bedrock, ROM). Bull Terriers as a breed are very special characters with charisma and a joie de vivre unmatched by any other breed. Bullies have always been a special favorite of mine, and Benson epitomized all the reasons that made them so. He had more fun at a dog show than any dog I've known.

Benson made many appearances in *Kennel Review*, the dog magazine I was publishing at the time, and, through him, I got to know many of the Bull Terrier people. Bull Terrier fans, like their dogs, are a breed unto themselves. Whereas most of the exhibitors I knew were in a lather about winning Groups and Bests in Show, Bull Terrier folks are more interested in good judging within their breed and find the real challenge in faring well amongst their own.

This attitude levels the playing field considerably and provides a far more stress-free approach to showing dogs. That said, when time and inclination permit (breeding always and raising puppies took priority), the Banbury dogs have done exceedingly well on all levels over the 35 years they've been shown. Between Banbury's first champion in 1968 and the most current in 2002, 117

Bull Terrier, Ch. Banbury Benson of Bedrock, along with his owner-handler, Mrs. Wingate Mackay-Smith, and a Benson puppy as they appeared on the cover of an issue of Kennel Review magazine that featured the owner-handler.

champions carry the "bred at Banbury" stamps of approval. Joining them have been 14 champions bred by others. These champions have accounted for Best of Variety or Best Opposite Sex at least 206 major entry National and Club Specialties. Winkie handled over 80 percent of these herself.

As one might expect of the introspective and low-key approach to showing dogs, Mrs. Mackay-Smith offers the following to those who choose to pursue handling their own dogs–things she wished she had known when she first began to show dogs:

• The results of judging are never life-threatening.

• Judges vary in their abilities, and their placing reflects this.

• A dog show is just that–a dog show and very unlike other livestock judging where conformation is the one and only criteria.

The Breeds, Groups, and Their Purposes

First and foremost, your most basic need for dog showing is a dog to show. Now, if you're serious about this–and you should be if you want to get full value from the time you're going to put in–you need a good dog. By that I don't mean a dog that behaves well; I mean a dog of *outstanding* quality. You can show any purebred and registered dog, but most people who show dogs would rather win than lose.

There are many books that go on at great length about what a show dog of any given breed should and shouldn't be. You will undoubtedly read a good many of them during your coming years, but because this book is aimed at your experience showing a dog, I want to make sure you

To succeed in dog showing, you need a dog of outstanding quality.

Your puppy's parents must be registered with the kennel club that is holding the event.

The breeder should be able to help you register your puppy.

understand how important quality is in your breed of choice.

In order to show your dog at an AKC dog show, your dog must come from a litter produced by both a sire and a dam that have been registered with that organization. This makes your dog eligible for registration as well.

Because you're purchasing a dog to show, you'll undoubtedly be dealing with people who show themselves. Therefore, the breeder of the litter will have handled all of the registration procedures correctly. However, the AKC can answer any questions you might have regarding registrations. All of the organization's contact numbers are located in the Resources at the end of this book.

You may not have even decided upon the breed of dog that you'd like to have yet. That's okay–you'll research the breeds and make the right decision for your family and lifestyle. There are 150-plus breeds that are currently being registered by the AKC. Let's take a look at what your choices are.

Making the Right Choice

The AKC gives full recognition to over 150 separate breeds of dogs, but that number increases as new breeds pass through what the AKC has named the Miscellaneous Class on their way to full recognition. The individual breeds are divided into the following seven categories or Variety Groups.

• Sporting

• Hound

The Shepherd (German)

Generally speaking, breeds are assigned to their respective Variety Groups based upon their origin and purpose. Though some breeds are multi-faceted and might be more popularly known for one characteristic, their initial origin and purpose dictates where they have been placed. The German Shepherd Dog is one example. The breed has gained worldwide respect as a guardian and protector, and those qualities have nearly obliterated the original intent of the breed. It would be natural to expect the German Shepherd to be found in the Working Group with other dogs that share guardian and protection duties, but the breed was originally developed to work livestock, as its name implies. For that reason, the German Shepherd is placed in the Herding Group.

Originally a herder, the German Shepherd has evolved into a protection and guard dog.

• Working

• Terrier

• Toy

• Non-Sporting

• Herding

The sporting dogs have natural hunting and retrieving instincts.

Sporting Group

The following breeds are included in the Sporting Group.

American Water Spaniel	Golden Retriever
Brittany	Gordon Setter
Chesapeake Bay Retriever	Irish Setter
Clumber Spaniel	Irish Water Spaniel
Cocker Spaniel	Labrador Retriever
Curly-Coated Retriever	Nova Scotia Duck Tolling Retriever
English Cocker Spaniel	Pointer
English Setter	Spinone Italiano
English Springer Spaniel	Sussex Spaniel
Field Spaniel	Vizsla
Flat Coated Retriever	Weimaraner
German Shorthaired Pointer	Welsh Springer Spaniel
German Wirehaired Pointer	Wirehaired Pointing Griffon

The Sporting Group

In a word, these are hunting dogs. In size, they run the gamut through large (the Retrievers), medium (the Spaniels), and small (the Cockers). There are breeds with long coats and others with short, smooth coats in this group. Some of them need little more than a hand glove and shine to get them ready for the ring, while others need extensive trimming and grooming. The breeds in this group are generally very amiable in temperament but do require some patience in living through their "puppyhood," which, in some breeds, can last until just before old age. As trying as their antics can be at times, it's hard not to love the sporting dogs because they seem to be born loving the world at large.

The Hound Group

With a notable exception or two, the Hound breeds are pretty well split down the middle between the sighthounds (breeds like Afghan Hounds, Salukis, Greyhounds, etc.) and the

A member of the Hound Group, Basset Hound Ch. Lil' Creek Briarcrest Top Gun, owned by Dan & Julie Jones, wins Group First at the prestigious Westminster Kennel Club dog show.

Sighthounds have the speed and agility to chase down prey.

Scenthounds follow the trail of their prey using their sense of smell.

The Hound Group

The following dogs are included in the Hound Group.

Afghan Hound	Harrier
American Foxhound	Ibizan Hound
Basenji	Irish Wolfhound
Basset Hound	Norwegian Elkhound
Beagle	Otterhound
Black and Tan Coonhound	Petit Basset Griffon Vendeen
Bloodhound	Pharoh Hound
Borzoi	Rhodesian Ridgeback
Dachshund	Saluki
English Foxhound	Scottish Deerhound
Greyhound	Whippet

scenthounds (Bassets, Beagles, Bloodhounds, etc.) How they do their job is indicated by their subdivision and is what creates the characteristics of that classification. Sighthounds, as their name indicates, look for their prey, and the scenthounds follow the scent trail that their prey leaves behind. The former is inclined to be exotic, not only in appearance but also in their approach to life. They have genuine likes and dislikes, and you'll find that their owners, more often than not, show only sighthounds. Sighthounds reserve their affection and respond best to their family. Scenthounds, on the other hand, are the good old boys of the Hound Group and will get along just fine with most anyone who'll provide a good meal and soft bed.

The Working Group

This group includes dogs whose heritage is based in guard and protection (for instance, Boxers, Doberman Pinschers, and the Mastiff breeds) or draught purposes. The latter include the dogs of Arctic derivative, like Samoyeds, Siberian Huskies, and Alaskan Malamutes. Although most of the super-sized breeds find home in this group, the newly

The Working Group

The following dogs are included in the Working Group.

Akita	Greater Swiss Mountain Dog
Alaskan Malamute	Komondor
Anatolian Shepherd Dog	Kuvasz
Bernese Mountain Dog	Mastiff
Boxer	Newfoundland
Bullmastiff	Portuguese Water Dog
Doberman Pinscher	Rottweiler
German Pinscher	Saint Bernard
Giant Schnauzer	Samoyed
Great Dane	Siberian Husky
Great Pyrenees	Standard Schnauzer

Working dogs, like the Akita, were bred to guard, protect, or assist their owners.

admitted German Pincher joins his working comrades measuring in at a 17-inch shoulder height. Some of these guys can be tough cookies, as the saying goes, and require a firm hand. They're smart dogs and know what they can and can't get away with.

The Terrier Group

Terriers can be nicely divided into three categories, depending upon the job for which the breed was originally developed. Simply put, the long-legged terriers (Fox Terriers, Kerry Blue Terriers, Irish Terriers, etc.) pursued their quarry. The short-legged terriers (Scotties, Westies, Cairns, etc.) "went to ground" (dug in) after their prey. The third category, the bull-and-terrier crosses, were originally bred as

The Terrier Group

The following dogs are included in the Terrier Group.

Airedale Terrier	Lakeland Terrier
American Staffordshire Terrier	Manchester Terrier
Australian Terrier	Miniature Bull Terrier
Bedlington Terrier	Miniature Schnauzer
Border Terrier	Norfolk Terrier
Bull Terrier	Norwich Terrier
Cairn Terrier	Scottish Terrier
Dandie Dinmont Terrier	Sealyham Terrier
Smooth Fox Terrier	Skye Terrier
Wire Fox Terrier	Soft Coated Wheaten Terrier
Irish Terrier	Staffordshire Bull Terrier
Jack Russell Terrier	Welsh Terrier
Kerry Blue Terrier	West Highland White Terrier

The top-winning Wire Fox Terrier of all time, Ch. Registry's Lonesome Dove, owned throughout her show career by Marion W. & Samuel Lawrence.

The toy breeds are known for their outgoing and playful dispositions.

fighting dogs, and although they, like any self-respecting terrier, will tolerate no guff from other dogs, the well-bred and properly raised members of this group are a delight to own and show. Although they make great show dogs capable of winning well, the coated breeds in this group require year-round expertise in preparing them for the show ring, and it is almost impossible to win with a terrier whose coat has not been perfectly prepared.

The Toy Group

These are the little guys of the dog world. Diminutive as they might be, they're the last to consider their own size. Most of them will take on a larger dog without batting one of their sparkling, little eyes. The toy breeds are great crowd pleasers because of their jaunty temperaments, and they provide a perfect option for someone who wants to show a

The Toy Group

The following dogs are included in the Toy Group.

Affenpinscher	Toy Manchester Terrier
Brussels Griffon	Miniature Pinscher
Cavalier King Charles Spaniel	Papillon
Chihuahua	Pekingese
Chinese Crested	Pomeranian
English Toy Spaniel	Toy Poodle
Havanese	Pug
Italian Greyhound	Shih Tzu
Japanese Chin	Silky Terrier
Maltese	Yorkshire Terrier
Toy Fox Terrier	

dog but doesn't have the strength or inclination to haul around a Great Dane or St. Bernard. Those who like coated breeds find favor with the toy breeds– although there's a coat to brush or perhaps to trim, it isn't like taking on the mega-task of preparing a Standard Poodle or Old English Sheepdog for the ring.

The Non-Sporting Group

This is the group that's really hard to categorize in that it's somewhat of a catchall. There's a size range of very small (Tibetan Spaniels) on up to very large (Standard Poodle) with every variation in between. There are coated breeds and smooth breeds, "love-the-world" types and those that only love their mommies or daddies.

The Non-Sporting Group is a mix of dogs of all shapes and sizes.

Here, it's a case of beauty being in the eye of the beholder, because even the shapes run the gamut from the Bulldog's stalwart frame to the sleek lines of the Dalmatian.

The Non-Sporting Group

The following dogs are included in the Non-Sporting Group.

American Eskimo Dog	Keeshond
Bichon Frise	Lhasa Apso
Boston Terrier	Löwchen
Bulldog	Poodle
Chinese Shar-Pei	Schipperke
Chow Chow	Shiba Inu
Dalmatian	Tibetan Spaniel
Finnish Spitz	Tibetan Terrier
French Bulldog	

The Herding Group

The following dogs are included in the Herding Group.

Australian Cattle Dog	Canaan Dog
Australian Shepherd	Cardigan Welsh Corgi
Bearded Collie	Collie
Belgian Malinois	German Shepherd Dog
Belgian Sheepdog	Old English Sheepdog
Belgian Tervuren	Pembroke Welsh Corgi
Border Collie	Puli
Bouvier des Flandres	Shetland Sheepdog
Briard	

The herding breeds were developed to work with livestock.

The Herding Group

It should come as no surprise that these breeds were all developed to work with livestock. Some are tall and some are short, but they all have very purposeful temperaments. They're fairly easy dogs to train for the ring, in general, and depending on how much you want to deal with hair, you can brush to your heart's content with an Old English Sheepdog or do a quick wipe-down with an Australian Cattle Dog.

The Miscellaneous Class

The AKC's interim Miscellaneous classification includes unrelated breeds being observed and processed prior to full AKC acceptance. Because this classification is primarily just a stopover, the breeds included are constantly changing. As of this writing, there are seven breeds included, and realistically, one has little to do with the other. Some people are fascinated with the rare breeds, but it should be

The Miscellaneous Class

Although the breeds are constantly changing, as of 2003, these breeds are included in the Miscellaneous Class.

Beauceron	Neapolitan Mastiff
Black Russian Terrier	Plotthound
Glen of Imaal Terrier	Redbone Coonhound

understood that the length of time that breeds spend in Miscellaneous varies considerably from a year or so on to a significant length of time. Breeds shown in Miscellaneous go no further than wins within their own breed and are not eligible to compete for Variety Group and Best in Show.

Selecting the Right Breed

There are many breeds that you can select, and there is no point in my making recommendations in that respect. As I've said, beauty is in the eye of the beholder, and once you've become involved with purebred dogs, you will be amazed at how your tastes can change.

I can clearly remember attending my first shows and wondering who could possibly want to own a Bull Terrier or a Whippet. Since then I've bred and shown Bull Terriers and find Whippets one of the breeds I enjoy judging best of all.

I only have one word of caution about selecting a dog to own or breed. Make sure that your choice is not based solely on what the breed looks like or its dazzling performance at a dog show. Bringing a dog into your home is

The breed you choose should fit in with your personality and lifestyle.

Part 1

Temperament should be of the utmost consideration when choosing a dog.

You and your show dog will spend a lot of time together, so make sure you get along.

commitment enough, but when you stop to think of all the additional hours a show dog shares with you, compatibility and upkeep become major considerations.

You may imagine yourself winning Best in Show at your local event with the Apollo of dogdom, the Great Dane, but if you live in a fifth-floor, walk-up, studio apartment, you're being naive as to how long that relationship is going to last. You'll either be forced to move to the country (at the strong suggestion of your landlord, if not by your own decision), or the two of you will develop a good case of claustrophobia. If you're allergic to dog hair or are a house-cleaning addict, think twice about a longhaired breed or any breed that sheds a great deal.

Do consider temperament. If the good life means calm and quiet to you, an off-the-wall, terrier-type doesn't sound like the perfect answer, regardless of how many blue ribbons the dog might bring home.

There are exceptions to the rules, of course, but don't depend on it. Make sure the dog or breed you select to launch yourself into show biz accommodates your lifestyle. The two of you are in the show ring an hour or so at a time and the days, weeks, and sometimes months in between can be long and agonizing if the two of you don't see life in the same manner.

The Fabled "Great One"

Each and every breed of dog has a written standard of perfection developed by experts in the breed. Breeders use this as the guideline by which they select their breeding stock, and judges use this to determine which are the best dogs in a given show ring. It stands to reason that within the confines of registered stock of any kind, there are going to be graduations of quality–poor, good, excellent.

It only stands to reason that stock consistently being graded as poor is highly unlikely to be the ideal candidate to produce stock of a caliber that would be graded excellent. This is nonetheless true in purebred dogs. Chances of obtaining superior quality out of mediocrity are less than remote. In breeding animals of any kind, achieving excellence is illusive, and to imagine doing so with inferior stock is out of the question.

Therefore, if you want to purchase foundation stock to breed show-quality dogs or simply purchase a dog to show, you should seek out those breeders who have earned a reputation for producing superior dogs over a long period of time. Even breeders who use the best stock available are being challenged, because they are

Seek out a breeder that has a reputation of producing superior dogs and past champions.

trying to breed what, in dog parlance, is referred to as a "great" one. Just like anything else in life, there is always a fast, faster, and fastest–good, better, and best. Purebred dogs are no different. Unlike what we believe to be true of humans–that all men and women are created equal–outside of the fact that they are all dogs, the canine world has some very clear-cut distinctions. Just because a dog is born of registered parents doesn't mean that he automatically has a future as a show dog.

What Makes a Great Show Dog?

I've been going to dog shows here in America most of my life. I've also had the opportunity to travel abroad and see the great dog shows of the world–Crufts in England, Goldfields in South Africa, and the Melbourne Royal in Australia, just to name a few. There were great show dogs at one time or another in all of those countries just as there have been here in America.

Those who saw the Lhasa Apso, Ch. Saxonspring's Fresno, win Best in Show over some 10,000 dogs at the world-famed Crufts Dog Show knew they were watching something that does not occur frequently. And so it was when I had the pleasure of awarding Best in Show to the Bull Terrier, Ch.

The Lhasa Apso, Ch. Saxonspring's Fresno, owned by Geoff Corrish.

Bull Terrier Ch. Hollyfir's Poachers Pocket of Piketburg was shown by his owner, Peet Oosthuizen, to Best in Show at South Africa's prestigious Goldfields' Dog of the Year Competition.

Troy Tanner and William Henery's Standard Poodle, Ch. Troymere Believe in Me, was shown to Best in Show by his owners at the Melbourne Royal, Australia's largest dog show.

Hollyfir's Poacher's Pocket of Piketberg, at South Africa's "Dog of the Year" competition in Johannesburg. Equally unforgettable was the great Standard Poodle, Australian Ch. Troymere Believe In Me.

Thinking about the many shows I've attended here in America and the many dogs I've seen at those shows, there are always those "unforgettable ones" that live so vividly in my memory. They come from among all breeds and the four corners of the country: In my early years it was the English Setter, Ch. Rock Falls Colonel. Later came the Whippet, Ch. Courtenay Fleetfoot of Pennyworth, who had been imported from England but took America by storm, climbing to the top at the country's most important events.

There have been great dogs in every class, dogs that are included in dogdom's Hall of Fame. Obviously, no one breed of dog has a lock on that unique category in which we place the very best, but the great dogs all share something special. That something is unique, yet it typifies each and every dog I've known that has earned distinction. It's that indefinable thing that perhaps finds its equal in a great stage performance or in coming upon a panoramic vista that makes your heart skip a beat. It's that something that

Part 1

William Holt's English Setter, Ch. Rock Falls Colonel, winner of 100 Bests in Show.

Margaret Newcombe's English import Whippet, Ch. Courtenay Fleetfoot of Pennyworth, who achieved American dogdom's triple crown: Westminster Kennel Club, International Kennel Club of Chicago, and Harbor Cities Kennel Club.

everyone who breeds and shows dogs hopes some day to have at the end of their show lead. It's that brass ring for which all of us play thegame.

What typified all of these dogs was their unique combination of charisma–star quality in attitude and deportment–and excellence in the characteristics called for in their respective breed standards. Some dogs stand out because of their charismatic qualities; others because they adhere so well to the attributes described in their standards. There are few, however, that have the good fortune to show superiority in both.

Although that extra something that great show dogs have is highlighted by a charismatic demeanor, there are some very real characteristics that they embody which makes them stand out from the masses. Each and every breed of dog has

Each breed of dog has a standard of excellence that describes the ideal.

Part 1

The search for the "perfect" dog is ongoing and keeps the sport new and interesting.

its standard of excellence that describes the ideal. The dogs who have earned the right to be classified among the greats of their breeds not only possess the characteristics outlined in their standard, but they also do so in such a high degree that some dog authorities are inclined to think of them as a fortunate accident.

This doesn't mean accidental in the sense that the unique combination of qualities comes about in an entirely haphazard fashion or the result of ancestors of no particular note. Even the very best breeding formulas, which employ superior bloodlines, are unable to produce or even reproduce with any accuracy what nature itself will occasionally allow to occur. Our best breeders live with the motto: "Breed the best to the best and hope for the best."

Great dogs are those one-in-a-million long shots for which everyone who breeds and shows dogs hopes and strives. The good breeder would love to have that icon of perfection appear in his or her next litter. Almost everyone that buys that next "show-prospect" puppy secretly fantasizes that this one will grow up to be the dream dog.

How often does that living embodiment of the standard come about? Rarely. The dog lives in our hopes and dreams far more often than it ever will in reality, but I do believe that trying to get there is really what keeps those of us involved on such a long-term basis. Perhaps that dream dog will appear in that next litter we breed, or that litter that we're going to take a look at next week.

It's no different than breeders of thoroughbred racing horses. They bring together the finest bloodlines the world has to offer–those backed up by individual stallions and mares known to be producers of winners. Does this guarantee they will have that Kentucky Derby winner they strive for? This is no guarantee of greatness, even from putting together the world's best, but you can rest assured that thoroughbred breeders have no illusions that the winner they hope for will come from breeding two nondescript plow horses together.

The Breed Standard

A great deal has been said about breed standards thus far and how important they are when determining where an individual dog might fall on the scale of excellence. A judge compares every dog in his ring against the respective breed's standard, and the breeder uses it as his or her ultimate road map to success in breeding. Because breed standards are such important tools, it behooves the beginner to understand where breed standards came from, what they were used for originally, and how they can best be used today.

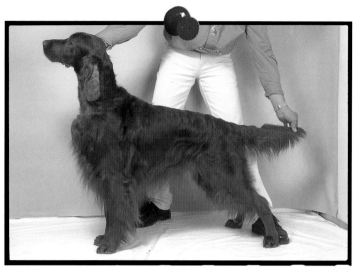

A judge compares every dog in the ring to the breed standard.

In order to do so, we have to go back in time to the beginning of human civilization. Even then a relationship between mankind and a beast of the forest had already begun to form. Back then, man's major pursuits were simply providing food for himself and his family and protecting the members of the tribe from the many dangers that threatened their existence. Many historians believe that early man saw many of his own social and survival efforts reflected in the habits of a particular animal–an animal that interestingly seemed to make increasing overtures at coexistence. That beast was none other than *Canis lupus*–the wolf.

Observation of the wolf could easily have taught early man some effective hunting skills

Dogs were originally pack animals but eventually came to rely on man for food and security.

that he, too, would be able to use advantageously. On a hunt, clever wolves did not single out the largest and boldest of a herd but worked as a team to bring down the weakest and most defenseless. Wolves saw in man's discards a source of easily secured food. The association grew from there.

The wolves that could assist man in satisfying the unending human need for food were of course most highly prized. It also became increasingly obvious as the man-wolf relationship developed through the ages that man could also use certain descendents of these increasingly domesticated wolves to assist in survival pursuits other than hunting.

Some of these wolves were large enough and strong enough to assist as beasts of burden. Others were aggressive enough to protect man's tribe from other less-friendly marauding beasts. It wouldn't have taken long to observe that wolf parents who were both adept at protecting the cave site were more apt to produce cubs that were similarly inclined than a wolf pair that couldn't give two howls who came or went.

The dogs that served man the best were bred to retain those useful characteristics.

As humans moved out of the caves and developed a more sophisticated and complex lifestyle, they found they could produce animals that could suit their new and specific needs from these descendants of the wolf. More often than not, this selective process was shaped by how and where man chose to live. Particular characteristics were prized, and breeding practices were used to both intensify desired characteristics and eliminate those that opposed the efficiency of the wolf descendents.

The herding wolves were selectively bred to retain their rugged constitution and their ability to round up their prey, but the prey instinct itself was, for all intents and purposes, eliminated. From still other descendants of the original wolf stock, man eliminated both the prey and herding instincts in favor of developing the manner in which members of the pack carried parts of the kill back to cubs waiting at the den.

As human settlements and encampments developed into towns and villages, life became easier, and mankind found time that could be devoted to pursuits other than simply staying alive. By this time, through selective breeding, man's personal wolves had evolved into a species so different they could be classified as *Canis familiaris* –domestic dog.

Meanwhile, throughout Europe, in order to keep the breeds' abilities to do their jobs, the owners of these dogs, who by this time could even be referred to as "fanciers," started to jot down the characteristics they believed were essential to performing a given task. What was written could well be considered the first breed standards. What was listed under those characteristics the breed should *not* have–the things that interfered with the breed's ability to perform–were the forerunners of today's breed faults.

The domestic dog evolved through the selective breeding of dogs that served a purpose.

At times, those involved in a breed found it necessary to cross their breed with another in order to perfect or add a specific characteristic. The outcrosses would occasionally bring in completely undesirable traits. At times, these undesirables were so offensive or so contrary to desired performance that they had to be eliminated at all costs. They required more than being designated simply as faults, and thus "Disqualifications" came about.

The checklists and guidelines contained in breed standards along with breed information that has been passed down through history help us see if the dogs being bred are going in the right direction–to see if they live up to the dictates of what has been intended for the breed. Granted, understanding what was intended and how it plays out in the dogs we have today isn't accomplished with a snap of the fingers. Through the years, even our most successful breeders and outstanding judges have pondered the degree of difficulty in doing so.

Part 1

The standard describes the physical and mental characteristics that distinguish the breed.

This was probably never better put than by England's Tom Horner, a brilliant breeder, judge, and dog writer of the last century. In discussing the complexity of dog standards he wrote:

"...there is more to this understanding of Standards than a mere ability to repeat them parrot-fashion. A child learns to repeat the Lord's Prayer, but it takes years for an adult full to understand its implications. To understand every requirement and implication of a Breed Standard takes time and application..."

Nevertheless, that process begins with first understanding what the standard aims to accomplish and some understanding of the terminology involved. All standards aim to preserve the characteristics that define the breed–the mental and physical characteristics that give the breed distinction, that separate it from all other breeds, and that allow it to fulfill its purpose. And it is critical to understand that all purebred breeds have a purpose. The purpose of some breeds is to protect. Other breeds provide a service–hunting, hauling, or entertaining. Still others accomplish their purpose in satisfying man's quest for beauty.

Let's use the official AKC Golden Retriever standard as an example and see what picture the many words intend to convey. It would be highly beneficial to have a good book of canine terminology handy when you read any standard, because there are terms that may be unfamiliar to the beginner or that may have a slightly different meaning within the canine vernacular. Each section of the breed standard is followed with an explanation of the standard written in italics.

Official Standard of the Golden Retriever

General Appearance – A symmetrical, powerful, active dog, sound and well put together, not clumsy nor long in the leg, displaying a kindly expression and possessing a personality that is eager, alert and self-confident. Primarily a hunting dog, he should be shown in hard working condition. Over-all appearance, balance, gait and purpose to be given more emphasis than any of his component parts.

Faults: Any departure from the described ideal shall be considered faulty to the degree to which it interferes with the breed's purpose or is contrary to breed character.

The General Appearance portion of breed standard aims to capture what I like to call "breed character," which I find to be a revealing key to the essence of a breed. Breed character is the immediate impression the dog gives at first sight. It tells you what to expect of the breed and whether or not the dog carries itself the way that specific breed is supposed to.

This section of the Golden Retriever standard describes a harmoniously constructed dog so nicely balanced so that no single part stands out above the rest. His powerful and athletic stature notwithstanding, the Golden's attitude and way of moving about are one of confidence and reliability. Even if you were to read no further than this in the Golden Retriever standard, you would already know what kind of a dog this is.

Size, Proportion, Substance – Males, 23-24 inches in height at withers; females, 21 ½–22 ½ inches. Dogs up to one inch above or below standard size should be proportionately penalized. Deviation in height of more than one inch from the standard shall disqualify.

Length from breastbone to point of buttocks slightly greater than height at withers in ratio of 12:11. Weight for dogs 65-75 pounds; bitches 55-65 pounds.

The purpose in giving these very specific measurements and proportions is to keep the Golden Retriever a medium-sized dog. Size and substance, along with relative proportions, tell a whole lot about how any dog will be able to perform. In the case of a Golden Retriever, too much size can take its toll on agility. On the other hand, if a Golden Retriever is too small or too short-legged, it may not be able to fulfill the duties of a dual-purpose land and water dog.

Head – Broad in skull, slightly arched laterally and longitudinally without prominence of frontal bones (forehead) or occipital bones. **Stop** well defined but not abrupt. **Foreface** deep and wide, nearly as long as skull. **Muzzle** straight in profile, blending smoothly and strongly into skull; when viewed in profile or from above, slightly deeper and wider at stop than at tip. No heaviness in flews. Removal of whiskers is permitted but not preferred.

The Golden Retriever is first and foremost a retrieving gun dog. The breed's head should be constructed in such a manner that it is powerful enough to pick up and carry land and water fowl of varying sizes. What is described here concerns itself with that ability.

Eyes – Friendly and intelligent in expression, medium large with dark, close-fitting rims, set well apart and reasonably deep in sockets. Color preferably dark brown; medium brown acceptable. Slant eyes and narrow, triangular eyes detract from correct expression and are to be faulted. No white or haw visible when looking straight ahead. Dogs showing evidence of functional abnormality of eyelids or eyelashes (such as, but not limited to, trichiasis, entropion, ectropion, or distichiasis) are to be excused from the ring.

Unimpaired vision is critical to a functional dog like the Golden Retriever, and the demands made by the standard make it obvious that anything that interferes with this ability are never to be condoned in the ring or in a breeding program.

Ears – Rather short with front edge attached well behind and just above the eye and falling close to cheek. When pulled forward, tip of ear should just cover the eye. Low, hound-like ear set to be faulted.

Nose – Black or brownish black, though fading to a lighter shade in cold weather not serious. Pink nose or one seriously lacking in pigmentation to be faulted.

Although the foregoing descriptions of eyes, ears, and nose have some functional purpose, they are primarily aesthetic

Most physical traits are established so that the dog can perform its original functions.

Body structure is an important aspect of the overall presentation of the dog.

concerns. *Minor variations are acceptable within these characteristics as long as they do not interfere with soundness and an ability to perform.*

Teeth – Scissors bite, in which the outer side of the lower incisors touches the inner side of the upper incisors. Undershot or overshot bite is a disqualification. Misalignment of teeth (irregular placement of incisors) or a level bite (incisors, meet each other edge to edge) is undesirable, but not to be confused with undershot or overshot. Full dentition. Obvious gaps are serious faults.

A detailed dental description and penalties for exceptions make it clear that dentition is important to the Golden Retriever. What humans do with their hands, dogs do with their mouths, and faults in this area could interfere with the Golden's ability to grasp and carry.

Neck, Topline, Body – **Neck** medium long, merging gradually into well laid back shoulders, giving sturdy, muscular appearance. Untrimmed natural ruff. No throatiness. **Backline** strong and level from withers to slightly sloping croup, whether standing or moving. Sloping back line, roach or sway back, flat or steep croup to be faulted. **Body** – well-balanced, short coupled, deep through the chest. **Chest** between forelegs at least as wide as a man's closed hand including thumb, with well developed forechest. Brisket extends to elbow. **Ribs** long and well sprung but not barrel shaped, extending well towards hindquarters. **Loin** short, muscular, wide and deep, with very little tuck-up. Slab-sidedness, narrow chest, lack of depth in brisket, excessive tuck-up, flat or steep croup to be faulted.

This section of the standard describes the overall silhouette of the Golden Retriever. Within that silhouette are the parts that enable the breed to perform as a retriever. A sturdy neck that also has sufficient length to be flexible enables the Golden to pick up and carry heavy water fowl. Solid body structure is an important requirement for a working retriever.

Tail – Well set on, thick and muscular at the base, following the natural line of the croup. Tail bones extend to, but not below, the point of hock. Carried with merry action, level or with some moderate upward curve; never curled over back nor between legs.

The Golden Retriever's tail is important for two different reasons: it serves as an indication of the dog's temperament, and it is used as a rudder when the dog is retrieving in water. The tail carried upright or curled over the back when other dogs are around can be a sign of aggressiveness. The tail tucked under the body indicates fear. Neither of these characteristics is desirable in the Golden Retriever.

Forequarters – Muscular, well co-ordinated with hindquarters and capable of free movement. Shoulder blades long and well laid back with upper tips fairly close together at withers. **Upper arms** appear about the same length as the blades, setting the elbows back beneath the upper tip of the blades, close to the ribs without looseness. **Legs,** viewed from the front, straight with good bone, but not to the point of coarseness. **Pasterns** short and strong, sloping slightly with no suggestion of weakness. Dewclaws on forelegs may be removed, but are normally left on. **Feet** medium size, round, compact and well knuckled, with thick pads. Excess hair may be trimmed to show natural size and contour. Splayed or hare feet to be faulted.

Hindquarters – Broad and strongly muscled. Profile of croup slopes slightly; the pelvic bone slopes at a slightly greater angle (approximately 30 degrees from horizontal). In a natural stance, the femur joins the pelvis at approximately a 90 degree angle; stifles well bent; hocks well let down with short, strong rear pasterns. Feet as in front. Legs straight when viewed from rear. Cow-hocks, spread hocks, and sickle hocks to be faulted.

As you read on through the standard, it should become increasingly obvious that soundness and serviceability are paramount. Sound legs and ruggedly constructed feet permit the Golden to work well on land and in water. The breed is admired for its beauty and amiable

The ideal dog should possess both soundness and serviceability.

The dog's correct coat should be functional as well as attractive.

Part 1

The color of the dog's coat helps to keep the breed recognizable.

temperament but judges and respected breeders are adamant that working ability always be given primary attention.

Coat – Dense and water repellent with good undercoat. Outer coat firm and resilient, neither coarse nor silky, lying close to body; may be straight or wavy. Untrimmed natural ruff; moderate feathering on back of forelegs and on underbody; heavier feathering on front of neck, back of thighs and underside of tail. Coat on head, paws and front of legs is short and even. Excessive length, open coats and limp, soft coats are very undesirable. Feet may be trimmed and stray hairs neatened, but the natural appearance of coat or outline should not be altered by cutting or clipping.

The correct Golden Retriever coat protects the dog in cold water and as he works his way through the brush and brambles on land. When of the correct texture, length, and density, the coat is functional and requires very little grooming to look attractive.

Color – Rich, lustrous golden of various shades. Feathering may be lighter than rest of coat. With the exception of graying or whitening of face or body due to age, any white marking, other than a few white hairs on the chest, should be penalized according to its extent. Allowable light shadings are not to be confused with white markings. Predominant body color which is either extremely pale or extremely dark is undesirable. Some latitude should be given to the light puppy whose coloring shows promise of deepening with maturity. Any noticeable area of black or other off-color hair is a serious fault.

Color has nothing to do with a dog's ability to work. Any shade of gold within the allowable spectrum is fully acceptable and constitutes nothing more than a matter of personal preference. That said, color preferences should never take precedence over correct breed type and working ability. The standard is clear as to what constitutes a color fault, i.e., white hairs other than on the chest and black or off-color hair. The aim is to keep the breed true to its name.

Gait – When trotting, gait is free, smooth, powerful and well co-ordinated, showing good reach. Viewed from any position, legs turn neither in nor out, nor do feet cross or interfere with each other. As speed increases, feet tend to converge toward center line of balance. It is recommended that dogs be shown on a loose lead to reflect true gait.

The true test of conformation is in a dog's movement. A dog that is constructed properly will, aside from an injury, almost invariably be able to move properly. Correct Golden Retriever movement should indicate strength, balance, and athleticism.

Temperament – Friendly, reliable and trust-worthy. Quarrelsomeness or hostility towards other dogs or people in normal situations, or an unwarranted show of timidity or nervousness, is not in keeping with Golden Retriever character. Such actions should be penalized according to their significance.

The true test of conformation is in a dog's movement.

A pleasant and compatible nature is a hallmark of the Sporting breeds. In order to be of value as a field dog, a Golden Retriever must be able to perform well in the company of other dogs and hunters other than his owner. These characteristics must carry over into every other walk of life the Golden encounters.

DISQUALIFICATIONS

Deviation in height of more than one inch from standard either way.

Undershot or overshot bite.

Disqualifications appear within the text of all breed standards and then again at the end of a standard to serve as another reminder of their importance. The AKC definition of disqualification is a decision made by a judge or bench show committee following a determination that a dog has a condition that makes it ineligible for further competition under the dog show rules or under the standard for its breed; an undesirable feature of a dog that results in such action.

Finding a Show Dog

Your chances of coming across the great one by accident are minimal at best. Can it happen that way? I suppose it can, but the question is, will it? Don't stand around waiting for that to happen to you. You might miss the boat waiting for your ship to come in.

Getting a dog of winning quality *is* within the realm of possibility. Do understand, however, that dog is most apt to come from one of two sources—an established and successful breeder of winning dogs or from your own breeding program. The latter comes following years of study, trial, and probably a whole lot of error.

Breeding Your Own Winner

There are many "how-to" breeding books written by people who have spent the best part of their lives learning how to do it. Can you skip all the preliminaries and just do as they say? I doubt it. You're not going to be able to produce worthy dogs of any breed unless you're capable of fully understanding what constitutes a top specimen.

You must educate yourself on your breed before you can choose a good show prospect.

Yes, you can read the standard of the breed—you can memorize it, in fact—but being able to recite a breed standard word for word has little bearing on fully understanding what those words imply. It is a never-ending process—a process that can hardly be accomplished in your beginning years.

Your initial years in dogs are about developing a foundation—learning the nuances of your breed, seeing where others have failed or succeeded. Look at this groundwork in the same light as you would view the medical student's undergraduate work. Those years are consequential and teeming with new knowledge and awareness. However, just as four years of undergraduate work come nowhere near qualifying the student for certification as a M.D., your introductory years probably cannot prepare you to know what an experienced breeder has invested an entire lifetime in learning.

Dog breeding entails great responsibility, and success comes after significant trial and error. It should be obvious that the individual who has the accumulated years of experience and familiarity with a breed is going to make far fewer mistakes than someone who has only an elementary foundation of knowledge with a breed. Remember that mistakes made in breeding are not disposable. The results can't be crumbled up and tossed in the wastebasket. The mistakes of breeding are living, breathing creatures that depend on the person who designed the breeding for their well-being and future care.

For those who do anticipate doing some breeding at some future point, I do have some advice I would like to share. When you set out to buy the dog that will mark your entry into the world of show dogs, think female and only female. (Actually you should be thinking bitch, because if you are going to get involved, that is the proper term for the female dog.)

The Importance of the Bitch

There is absolutely nothing more important to a small breeding program than starting with a well-bred bitch of high quality. After her show career, you can then go on to select the most suitable sire for her. When I say "most suitable," I mean the male who will complement her quality in that he will assist her in producing puppies that pass on her good characteristics but also add his good qualities that she might lack.

Even if that first breeding doesn't produce the winner

Dog breeding is a big responsibility and should only be done by those with experience and knowledge.

It takes years of practice and observation to fully understand a breed standard.

A Show Dog "Campaign"

Normally speaking, the owner or handler will show their dog at shows in convenient locations or at shows where the judge might see the exhibitor's dog in a favorable light. A show dog "campaign," on the other hand, means a dog is being shown to achieve some particular standing like "Number One in the Breed" or "Top Sporting Dog." The campaign usually entails extensive showing—often every weekend of the year—in order to make sure that the dog stands well ahead of its competition in accumulative wins. Unlike past methods, today's campaigns also involve extensive advertising in the magazines devoted to winning dogs. Even when the owner himself undertakes the campaign, it is a costly venture. Travel by air and by car, hotels, entry fees, and advertising add up to a significant figure that make it clear that a show dog campaign differs radically from simply showing a dog "for the fun of it!"

you hoped for, there are other outstanding stud dogs available. A different combination of bloodlines might be just the ticket the next time around.

Even if you decide to limit a foundation bitch to one litter, the option exists to keep one of her best daughters to show and continue the breeding program. In other words, starting with a bitch gives the beginner options.

Purchasing a female will give you more options in your breeding program.

The options are not as readily available if the first purchase is a male. The possibility of a novice buying a top-level male to begin a showing and breeding program with is both unlikely and limiting. A serious breeder who does produce an exceptionally promising young male is going to be reluctant to place the dog with a beginner. Truly outstanding males are extremely difficult to come by, and in many (but not all) breeds, they are best suited to extended show ring campaigns.

Although many "good" male dogs are born to well-bred litters, the only ones that other breeders or individuals who show dogs are interested in are the potentially "great" ones. Not many breeders would risk the gamble of putting something that is so hard to come by and in such high demand in the hands of someone with little or no experience.

Males of this caliber deserve the advantages of a well-thought-out career in the show ring. A good part of that career is having the dog presented at shows by someone who has the handling ability commensurate with the dog's quality. You'll get a clearer picture of just how important that is as we move along in this book.

The question that might then arise is why not start with a male of lesser quality—one that does not require all that special attention and experience? The answer becomes apparent, as we look at the next steps in a planned breeding program.

Show-quality puppies are hard to find—be selective when choosing from a litter.

There are good many reasons why starting with even the best of males limits the small hobby breeder-exhibitor. Even in the event that the beginner should defy the odds and handle the dog to a highly successful show career, the time comes when the breeding program must begin.

Although the novice who began with the good bitch has his or her choice of any stud dog in the country that properly compliments the bitch (known as breeding up), the owner of the male must go out and buy the proper mate for the male. If the beginner has the good fortune of owning a superior quality male, the search will not be quite as difficult. However, if the male is of "average" quality, it would not make good sense to scour the country

Buying a show-quality puppy to start your breeding program is the fastest way to succeed.

Spend time observing the breed you are interested in before you purchase a puppy.

for a top-quality foundation bitch only to breed her to a dog of only average quality (known as breeding down).

Buying Your First Show Dog

Obviously, a person who has just become interested in dog shows is not going to have the background to begin a breeding program that will produce show dogs of winning quality off the bat. The sensible thing to do is to *buy* that first quality show dog and go on from there.

Ideally, a beginner would invest quite a lot of time reading, studying, and observing the rights and wrongs of the breed he or she might be interested in. This would provide time to learn at least some of the things the "old timers" in a breed have invested a lifetime in acquiring.

But who wants to wait around for all that? If you want it now, why not have it now? Unfortunately, there's danger in that kind of thinking. Beginners are inclined to get started somewhere near the middle–owning any number of average quality dogs–before they realize what they *should have* done was begin with just one really good dog.

In order to recognize a winning show dog, attend as many dog shows as possible.

Restraint, patience, self-control, and resolve–call all those virtues into play if you can. The more time you spend observing the breed of your choice at dog shows, the more likely that first purchase will be a sound one. Read and attend as many shows as possible. Discuss the breed with those who seem to have the winning dogs. Eventually you will be able to recognize the subtle, and at times not so subtle, differences that exist in the good, better, and best of a breed.

You'll also begin to find that there are some breeders who consistently produce more winners than their competitors. These are the people that you should try to get to know well. Most successful breeders who determine that you are sincere in becoming involved in their breed–in possibly becoming a breeder or an exhibitor–will bend over backward to help you. If you can locate someone like this to act as your mentor, it's worth every minute of the time you invest in doing so.

When starting out, pick a mentor with experience in the breed and follow his or her advice.

I assure you that following in the footsteps of a respected and successful individual in your early years in dog showing is one of the most important choices you can make. Once you learn how it's all been accomplished in the past, you'll be more readily equipped to try some well-thought-out experimenting on your own because you'll have a sound foundation to rely upon.

In many cases, working with the guidance of a mentor will mean attending shows with them and learning in advance how to avoid many of the normal pitfalls and blunders novices are inclined to make. We all learn by doing, of course, but having warning of problem areas ahead of time can save a lot of embarrassing moments that are better invested in learning the right way to do something.

If you're very clear in stating what you hope to do with the dog you are purchasing, good breeders are inclined to go out of their way to make sure they help you do just that. After all, they are obviously devoted to their breed. They've hung in there through the years, and if they believe you are a

A co-ownership can be a good way to get started in dog showing.

candidate to carry on what they've worked so hard to accomplish, they're more than happy to assist.

Co-Ownerships

It is not at all unusual for a breeder to have a dog of show potential in their kennel that they may not be ready to sell outright because it may somehow figure into their future breeding plans. They may, however, not be averse to letting someone they have confidence in become a "co-owner" of the dog.

There are many ways that this can be arranged, but what it usually means is that the interested buyer and the breeder own the dog jointly. The co-owner is permitted to keep and show the dog, but legal ownership is shared. This ownership information appears in the show catalog at every show in which the dog is entered.

If you decide to co-own a dog, clarify each parties' responsibilities in a written contract.

This is obviously not bad publicity for the new co-owner. The ownership arrangement suggests the breeder thinks enough of the dogs to want to maintain some degree of say in its future. It also implies that the known breeder has confidence and trust in the unknown new co-owner.

Responsibilities, financial and otherwise, should always be outlined in a written contract that is signed by both parties involved in the co-ownership transaction. All restrictions and responsibilities of either party should be itemized. This avoids any conflicts or questions at a later date.

Even though both parties may be good friends, a written contract is still very important. Samuel Goldwyn, Hollywood film mogul and referred to by many in the industry as "master of the malaprop," is often quoted as having said, "A verbal contract isn't worth the paper it's written on!"

The passing of time itself can make verbal agreements open to argument, and the death of one of the partners can create questions on the part of the decedent's heirs. A well-written contract listing any and all eventualities and agreed upon by everyone concerned is usually the beginning of a sound and fruitful co-ownership.

Another suggestion I have is for the contracts to conclude at a specific point in time. In other words, once the outlined conditions have been met by both or one of the parties, the dog involved will become the sole property of one or the other in the agreement. Endless co-ownerships can lead to complicated legal entanglements that can be avoided by bringing the contract to a close at some point in time.

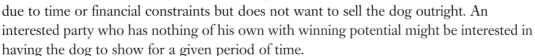

Another option is to lease a dog from a breeder or owner.

Leasing

Arrangements can also be made to lease a dog from a breeder or another owner. Occasionally the breeder of a dog is unable to show a quality dog due to time or financial constraints but does not want to sell the dog outright. An interested party who has nothing of his own with winning potential might be interested in having the dog to show for a given period of time.

A lease agreement can be arranged by obtaining a form from the AKC that requests the terms and the names of the individuals that are involved in the lease. This form is filed with the AKC and becomes a matter of their official records for the term of the lease.

Legal ownership of the dog remains with the lessor while the lessee has the right to show or breed the dog concerned as if it were his or her own during the time and under the conditions of the lease in so long as the terms of the lease are maintained. Any contingencies are, of course, outlined in an agreement signed by the parties involved. Again, the lease should always have a beginning and end date.

A beginner should start out with the best dog possible and learn from each competition.

Someone beginning in dogs can benefit immensely by leasing a dog from a breeder-mentor and there are many ways that this can be accomplished. It only makes sense, however, that an exchange of money or, in this case, dogs, is always accompanied by all the necessary procedures and documents that make the lease transaction a legal one.

What to Expect

Any registered purebred dog *can* be shown, but the foregoing will undoubtedly make it clear that not all of them *should be* shown. Long-time breeders understand that breeding top quality even from the very best bloodlines is no simple task. They also know that attempting to produce winning quality from mediocre stock is an exercise in futility.

It takes top-notch stock in order to win consistently under the best of conditions. Needless to say, the beginner cannot offer a dog what the experienced exhibitor can in the way of in-ring technique. Therefore, it is tantamount to a beginner's success that he enter the ring with as good a dog as he can possibly obtain to help bridge the gap that stands between himself and the more experienced competition.

Once in the ring, however, the novice has to understand the presiding judge is governed by a strict schedule. There is not a great deal of time available for the judge to struggle through the beginner's poor presentation to find a dog's qualities. Preparing yourself and your dog to be seen to advantage is the next important step along the road to success, and the following chapter is devoted to just that.

Getting Your Dog Ready for the Ring

So, you've gone to the top (or as close as you could get) and bought the dog with the bluest blood known to the free world. You're now the proud owner of that wonder pup you dreamed about. All the work is done, and the two of you are ready to burn up the show ring, right?

Getting a great dog is the prime place to start, but I assure you there is a whole lot more to winning than simply owning a top-quality dog. In athletics, an individual's genetic makeup provides the potential. What an athlete does with that potential determines how successful he or she will be in the pursuit of the gold. Show dogs are no different.

A top-quality show dog is just the beginning—now the real work starts.

All show dogs must first be healthy, well-conditioned athletes.

Your dog must look and feel his best to succeed in the show ring.

Even the Olympiad's greatest gold medal contender would be forced out of competition if he or she didn't remain in the peak physical and mental condition. The combination of physical and mental health, regular conditioning, and an effective training regimen is what it takes to get to the top.

"Athlete?" You're probably asking yourself, "Peppe, my Chihuahua, is an athlete?" or "Norton the Newfie, that big lug stretched out on the sofa, is an *athlete?*"

Plain and simply–yes. That is, if Peppe and Norton are show dogs.

Soundness, coat condition, muscle tone–the whole works–count in the dog game, and in more ways than even some long-time exhibitors understand. Though it's our responsibility as dog owners to keep any dog we own healthy and fit, doing so becomes particularly important in the case of dogs we might want to breed or show.

The responsibility of the dog judge is to select the stock most suitable to maintain quality and improve the breed. The judge's decisions are based upon both the written and unwritten standard. The written standard states, or at least implies, that the dog should be mentally sound–a good canine citizen. The written standard is also the primary source for the physical characteristics of a given breed. It's a description of a dog's anatomical parts and how the parts should fit together. The unwritten standard is the one that demands that a show dog be sound, healthy, and well conditioned. The latter is very often a determining factor in close-call decisions.

Good breeding determines whether or not your Greyhound, Poodle, or Boxer is a quality representative of the breed. However, if your dog spends his life lounging on a chaise lounge, his muscle tone, stamina, coordination, and foot timing will suffer severely, and the dog may become incapable of performing in the manner for which the breed was created.

Keeping your dog fit and well-exercised is very important.

This is true for all the breeds, even the decorative toy dogs. Keep in mind that the judge is looking for excellence. When it gets down to keen competition–even if two outstanding dogs were identical in every other respect–the more physically fit of the two would prevail.

The top professional handlers who are campaigning dogs for the big awards are often on the road or flying back and forth across the country for weeks, sometimes months, on end. They know it is absolutely impossible to achieve the condition and muscle tone required of their top-level dogs with a few quick turns around the show ring on weekends.

Keeping the dogs in condition is as important to the professionals as learning how to properly groom and present the dogs in the ring. Many of these professionals do not have the luxury of returning home after each event, as does the owner-handler. The owner-handler usually comes home on a Sunday night after a weekend of shows and, after perhaps a day of rest, is busy doing road work, using a treadmill, or involved in whatever the physical activity is that best suits the breed of dog.

Exercise is an essential part of a show dog's daily routine.

The professional, on the other hand, is probably packing his motor home in Miami Beach on the morning after a weekend of shows. Once all the gear is safely stored, the dogs fed and exercised, it's off to Chicago, St. Louis, or an exotic port of call for the shows that will begin the following Friday.

Does the professional try and squeeze by without the all-important conditioning a show dog must have? Certainly not the successful professional. Rare circumstances might interfere with exercise every once in a while during a campaign, but a savvy handler won't make this a habit. Professionals know that allowing that to happen frequently minimizes a dog's chances to win significantly.

When the handler does arrive at the next set of shows and sets up all the necessary equipment, the dogs are fed and given time to relieve themselves and then the real work begins. Out come the walking shoes or bicycle and around the fairgrounds or outside the perimeters of the show site the handler or the handler's assistant go, the dog happily by his or her side.

Peddling to the Top

In the two-year period covering 1993 and 1994, professional handler Jimmy Moses handled the German Shepherd Dog Ch. Altana's Mystique to 205 All-Breed Bests in Show. That remarkable record not only made her the top-winning dog of all breeds for those two years, but her accumulative total also made her the top-winning dog of any breed of all time.

To truly appreciate those accomplishments, you have to consider that the two-year period included approximately 104 two-or-three-show weekends. This put Moses and Mystique away from home *at least* every Friday through Monday weekend of those two years!

What makes it really amazing, however, is that, in addition to her great type and construction, Mystique was always shown in magnificent condition. The luster of her coat was obvious even from ringside, and, as she moved around the ring, the muscularity and power so important to that breed created standing ovations from observers.

Moses flew commercial airlines to most of the shows where Mystique was entered. There was always a good deal of equipment that accompanied the team from show to show, and

Backstage Photo

Professional handler Jimmy Moses handled the German Shepherd Dog
female, Ch. Altana's Mystique, to a phenomenal record of over 200
All-Breed Best in Show wins, a campaign which kept them on the road
constantly for almost two years.

Part 1

Bicycling is a great way to keep your dog in tip-top shape.

Always consider your dog's breed and activity level before starting an exercise regimen.

an important part of the equipment was a fold-up bicycle that they worked out on every single day that they were not at home.

Common sense applies here, naturally. The kind of exercise a German Shepherd requires to remain in top-notch shape is not suitable for a Pug. The complex breathing system of a Bulldog prohibits any kind of exercise in hot and humid weather, and good judgment tells us a little Chihuahua will not survive a forced march through snow drifts in sub-zero temperatures.

That said, it's up to the owner to determine how and when his or her dog can be properly exercised. Some of the dogs in the Toy and Terrier Groups are so active that their constant household patrols and hair-trigger responses keep them in fine fettle. However, in dogs of just about any breed, there are the born couch potatoes. Don't assume that because Peppe the Chihuahua has a ten-bedroom house to patrol or because Big Red the Irish Setter has a whole yard to chase imaginary rabbits in that they will do so.

Without another dog around that is very pro-active about exercise, you'll find most dogs become less and less inclined to be self-starters. It's always best to supervise your show dog's exercise, that way you'll be sure the dog is getting enough of the right kind.

Fortunately, you do not have to become a marathon runner to give your dog the exercise he needs. Walking at a pace that keeps your dog moving at a steady trot (not a gallop!) over a sensibly extended period of time is the best possible kind of exercise you can give your dog.

Age-Appropriate Exercise

Exercise must be geared to the age of the dog you are conditioning. What's appropriate for the young adult at the prime of his life can be harmful to the young puppy or fatal to the older dog.

Puppy Exercise

If you watch puppies at play with their littermates, you will note that there are frequent, but brief, bouts of high-level activity. This is nearly always followed by a good, long nap. Puppies need exercise, but only as much as they prefer, and then they should be given ample time to rest.

Some breeds are very deceiving in that they reach full height and develop luxurious coats by the age of six to seven months. However, do not to judge this as "maturity," because it is only skin deep. Inside that tall frame and lavish coat is the developing body of a baby. Forced exercise, even short periods of jogging on pavement, can permanently damage the growing bones and muscles of a young dog, and I seriously advise you to proceed with caution and restraint until your developing youngster is at least 12 to 18 months of age.

This doesn't mean the two of you have to sit on the sofa waiting for your dog's first birthday to get moving. Easy, sensibly timed periods of exercise will keep your dog in fine shape until he requires an adult workout program.

Beware of Bloat

Veterinarians caution against feeding immediately before or after strenuous exercise, as they believe it definitely can lead to bloat, a condition that affects many breeds, particularly the medium-large through giant breeds. Bloat, or gastric torsion, is a condition where gases are produced in great amounts and may result in the twisting of the stomach. Bloat can cause extreme pain, and, in most cases, death without immediate treatment.

Puppies need equal amounts of exercise and rest—be sure to keep your pup from overdoing it.

Start your exercise program slowly and increase it gradually.

Exercise for Young and Mature Adults

Once out of puppyhood, your dog will probably be able to out-walk you any day of the week and still have energy left over for aerobics. Starting a new exercise program for your dog requires that you do so gradually, however, and you should increase the duration very slowly. If you live near a lake, many breeds love to swim, and there couldn't be any better exercise. Any place that is safe for you to swim will be safe for your dog as well. However, don't throw your dog out into the middle of the lake for the first test swim. Some breeds (Bulldogs and Bull Terriers for sure) have the aquatic ability of millstones, so be on hand and in shallow water for those first few tryouts.

On the one hand, a swimming pool offers you more control, but all swimming pools are chlorine treated and chlorine can be anathema to a dog's coat. It can bleach out the blacks and dark colors and make other colors turn peculiar shades of green and auburn. Proceed with caution.

Not all dogs' musculature is obvious to the eye because of their construction or wealth of coat. Don't mistake fat for muscle. It is up to you to keep your show dog in *real* show condition.

Anatomy 101

Involvement in purebred dogs requires that you have at least a basic understanding and a working familiarity with canine anatomy. If a judge says he put your Fido fourth in a class of four because his brisket wasn't deep enough, you can't afford to think this has something to do with what kind of meat your dog ate the night before.

I'm not going to try and give you a course in basic canine anatomy here, but having a good grasp on

Swimming is an excellent and enjoyable way to exercise most breeds of dog.

correct terminology is important if you're going to be involved in showing dogs. Remembering as many of the basic parts and where they're located will serve you well at shows and with your veterinarian. The parts named apply to all breeds of dog. Each breed has its own shape, but dogs are dogs, and the basic principals of canine anatomy apply to them all, giant or toy.

Anatomy Road Map

Nose: The external cartilage and nasal cavity.

Muzzle: The foreface of the dog, including the upper and lower jaw and nose portion of the head.

Skull: The bone components of the head. This includes the braincase and muzzle.

Eyes: The eyeballs and eyelids. The shape of the surrounding tissue and eyelid determines the eye shape as described in breed standards.

Ears: The organ for hearing, including the external lobe. There are many different kinds of ears for different breeds, including erect, butterfly, drop, and folded ears.

Stop: The dividing line between the muzzle and the skull.

Occiput: The back portion of the skull where the neck muscles attach themselves to the skull.

Neck: The part located between the head and the shoulders.

Crest: The arched part of the neck located below the occiput.

Shoulders: Shoulder blade and muscles surrounding the area.

Just Where Is a Dog's Back?

Anatomy experts say that only a small portion of the area that extends between a dog's withers and the set on of tail is actually the back. In anatomical terms, the back is that portion of the topline that begins at a point just behind the withers and ends at the junction of the loins and croup. But because this is your introductory course, I'll let you have that discussion directly with the anatomical experts who like to be absolutely precise. If you refer to the whole area between withers and tail as "the back," everyone will understand exactly what you mean.

Part 1

Akita Ch. The Widow-Maker O'BJ (ROMXP), an outstanding winner and producer of champions, owned by B.J. Andrews.

Part 1

Ch. Beau Monde Miss Chaminade, bred and owned by the author and Barbara B. Stubbs.

A familiarity of canine anatomy will help you to understand the breed standard.

Withers: The junctures at the top of the shoulder blades.

Tail: The end portion of a dog's spinal column.

Pelvis: The bones attached to the spinal column between the tail and the loin, which provide sockets for both of the rear legs.

Forelegs: The front legs.

Pastern: The area between the wrist and the forefoot.

Forearm: The area between the wrist and the elbow that hooks to the uppers arm and connects to the bottom edge of the shoulder blade.

Loin: The area on the side of the dog between the rib cage and the pelvic area.

Back: The part of the spine that extends between the withers and the loin.

Dewclaws

The standards of some breeds require the presence of dewclaws. Breeds like Briards require dewclaws on the rear legs—the Briard must be disqualified from competition by the judge if it has "less than two dewclaws on each rear leg" They are optional on the front legs of the Briard. Absence of double dewclaws on the rear legs is considered a fault of the Great Pyrenees and single dewclaws are asked for in the front as well.

The breed standard of the Chesapeake Bay Retriever requires that any dog that has dewclaws on its rear legs be disqualified from competition. However, dewclaws on the front legs are optional and may or many not be removed.

It is important to know what the standard of your breed has to say in respect to dewclaws. Don't panic if your dog doesn't have them, because those that breed dogs that aren't required to have dewclaws usually remove them or have them removed by their veterinarian just a few days after the puppies are born.

What "Soundness" Means

When all the parts of a dog hang together correctly so the dog is able to move easily as a collected unit, the dog is referred to as being "sound." At shows, dogs are required to "gait" (that is, to move around the ring) at a trot. Their degree of soundness is evaluated when they are moving. That said, it's important to understand that not all breeds of dog move exactly alike nor do they move at the same speed. It is extremely important for the person showing a dog to understand what a given breed's proper movement looks like and to adjust the speed at which the dog moves to have the dog look its best, which we'll learn more about later in the book.

Hips: The pelvic girdle that provides for the attachment of the dog's rear legs.

Croup: The area that extends from above the loin area to the base of the tail.

Stifle joint: The knee joint.

Hock joint: The lower joint on the rear leg parallel to the ground.

Upper thigh: The area between the hip joint and the stifle joint.

Lower thigh: The area between the stifle joint and the hock joint.

Pads: The soft material on the underside of a dog's feet.

Buttocks: The muscular area below the croup and above the rear legs.

Rear pastern: Area from the hock joint to the paw.

Dewclaws: Unused fifth toe on the inside of both the front and rear legs.

Dewclaw Removal

Dewclaws are the extra or functionless (vestigial) digit that may be located on the inside of the legs just above the foot. Removal is a simple procedure best performed by a veterinarian with sharp manicure-type scissors within a few days of birth. The protruding dewclaw is removed at its base, removing no more skin than necessary. When performed properly, sutures are seldom required in that so little skin is removed. However, many vets cauterize the area with silver nitrate.

Regular vet checkups can help prevent many health conditions.

Health Watch

Anyone who has visited his or her own doctor or who has had even the briefest hospital stay is aware of the high cost of medical care. Our dog's medical bills may not be quite as high as our own, but they aren't inexpensive by any means.

Although showing dogs might not be as expensive a hobby as keeping racehorses or competitive sailing, it's expensive enough. A good amount of the causes for costly veterinary treatment can be prevented by greater diligence in home care and regular veterinary checkups. The old saying about an ounce of prevention being worth a pound of cure certainly applies here.

It's easy to forget to look at certain parts of your dog's anatomy as you go through your busy life. However, neglecting to do so over extended periods of time can allow minor problems to develop into situations that require prolonged veterinary care and expensive surgery, not to mention surgery that may bar your dog from ever being shown.

A smart idea is to create a checklist containing all the things you should be looking for as you groom your dog (see Weekly Home Care Checklist.) Post that where you normally groom your dog so that you can glance at it while you're brushing or trimming.

Your Dog's Veterinarian

Athletes have their professional sports medicine practitioners; your dog has his veterinarian. Your vet will help you determine if your dog is healthy enough to get into proper condition. Good breeding and good health allow a dog to get in top physical shape. Regular veterinary checkups will keep your dog in the state of health that will allow you to pursue the steps that add up to top conditioning.

There is no one who knows more about the best veterinarian than the breeder from whom you purchased your dog. If you are fortunate enough to live in the same area, your problems are solved. You can continue right on with the vet that has known your puppy since birth.

Unfortunately, that may not be possible because of distance, and I do recommend that you have a veterinarian that you can get to in a hurry. As good as any veterinarian might be, if he or she lives hours away and you have an emergency situation, it may cost your dog his life.

Still, your breeder may be able to help by having friends or fellow dog breeders in your area provide recommendations. It's a good idea to pay a visit to the recommended hospital ahead of time. Inspect the premises and discuss the care of your breed with the vet.

Your vet is your dog's best friend and can help keep him healthy and sound.

If the facility and the person you speak to meet your approval, make an appointment to take your dog there for his first checkup. Although it may not always be possible, the ideal

Weekly Home Care Checklist

1. Check skin for eruptions.

2. Thoroughly brush his coat to eliminate dead hair and debris.

3. Make sure ears are always clean without offensive odor.

4. Check that teeth are white without accumulated tartar. Brush regularly only with cleansing products made for dogs.

5. Check that eyes are clear and bright with no discharge or irritation.

6. Inspect nails to be sure there are no cracks, and keep them trimmed to appropriate length.

7. Check anal glands (sacs located on each side of the dog's anus) to make sure they are not impacted.

8. Check anal temperature whenever your dog appears out of sorts. Normal is between 101.5 and 102° F.

Your breeder can recommend a reputable vet in your area.

Try to make your dog's vet visits as positive as possible.

situation is to have your dog seen by the same veterinarian each time you take your dog to that hospital. Some clinics have several veterinarians in attendance, and it becomes the luck of the draw as to who will see your dog.

Why do I consider this important? Some dogs just flat out hate going to the vet's office. Even if nothing adverse has ever happened there, each visit is a traumatic one for them. For dogs with this problem, being treated by a complete stranger each time they have to visit the veterinary hospital can be just enough to make a bad situation absolutely impossible.

Blossom, our Chow Chow, had extremely definite likes and dislikes–particularly with people (which made showing her a guessing game at best). It was she who decided who would and would not treat her at the clinic we used. Some of the vets and technicians she absolutely adored, and others she disliked.

Anyone who has had experience with the breed knows that when a Chow makes up his mind on something, that is *exactly* how it's going to be, and there is little, if any, room for mediation. So Blossom could only go to the veterinarian's on the day her chosen few were in attendance.

Your veterinarian, accustomed to dealing with your breed of dog, knows best. I cannot caution you strongly enough regarding the importance of using a veterinarian who has had experience with your breed.

Each breed has its own constitutional and health-related peculiarities, and a veterinarian, as well schooled as he or she may be, may not be aware of these idiosyncrasies. For instance, Weimaraner breeders are emphatic about the number of inoculations that can be given their breed at any one time. They are also adamant about the time that must elapse between the necessary inoculations. Failing to follow experienced Weimaraner breeders' recommendations for their breed in this respect may result in permanent injury to the dog, sometimes death. Not all vets know everything about all breeds. Use a vet recommended by someone in your breed and, whenever possible, use a vet who has had some experience with show dogs.

It may be perfectly all right to shave the hair off old retired Rover's leg for a shot, but not so great to do the same to the dog you plan on taking to a show the next day or next week. The show-dog-savvy vet will ask about such things or automatically administer treatment in an area of the dog's anatomy that will be as unnoticeable as possible.

Use a vet that has experience with your breed and with show dogs.

Inherited Health Problems and Diseases

All breeds of domesticated dogs, and even some mixed breeds, have hereditary problems. Because of this, reputable breeders rigidly test and cull their breeding stock to avoid these problems as much as possible. Breeders do their utmost to breed around inheritable problems. That said, breeders are not perfect. Occasionally, complications can arise in even the best-planned breeding.

Understandably, veterinarians do not want you to perpetuate health problems when they do exist. Often, they will recommend spaying or neutering when they encounter these genetic difficulties. In most cases, their advice is sound. However, a word to the wise in this

All breeds of dog have heredity problems that can be controlled through good breeding.

Inherited Diseases

Bone Disorders:

Hip dysplasia— This is an orthopedic problem that affects many breeds of dog. It is a malformation of the hip joints that, in its advanced stages, can seriously affect movement.

Canine elbow dysplasia—This condition results when the three bones of the elbow (radius, ulna, and humerus) do not knit together properly in puppyhood. The degree to which this has not properly developed determines the extent of harm it does to movement.

Osteosarcoma—The most common bone cancer in dogs, particularly those weighing over 50 pounds.

Patella luxation—Commonly referred to as slipping stifles, this condition of the knee joint leads to dislocation of the kneecap and is particularly prevalent in small breeds.

Tumors:

Benign tumors—Skin tumors are common in some breeds. Most are benign, appearing randomly on the body, but do not spread by invading healthy organs. Although they are benign, they do increase in size and can seriously affect the dog's appearance.

Cancerous tumors—Cancerous tumors can spread into adjacent areas of the body, or they may release cells to form secondary tumors in other organs. Possible treatment includes removal through surgery, chemotherapy, and radiotherapy.

Eye Disorders:

Entropion—This is a condition of the eye where the eyelids turn inward, causing the eyelash to rub on the surface of the eyeball, irritating the eye, and, in extreme cases, damaging the eyeball itself. This condition is best dealt with by corrective eye surgery performed by an experienced veterinary surgeon.

Ectropion—Ectropion is a condition in which the lower eyelids droop, turning outward, and create a pocket in which debris can accumulate. This condition is best dealt with by corrective eye surgery performed by an experienced veterinary surgeon.

Cataracts—This is a degenerating condition of the part of the eye directly behind the pupil, which becomes fully or partially opaque, giving it a milky or blue color. Extremely expensive surgery is the only known corrective measure.

respect: Once a bitch is spayed or a male neutered, the procedure can never be reversed, nor can that dog or bitch ever be shown other than in classes designed and specifically designated to include sexually altered individuals. Here again, discussing the problem and the vet's recommendations with an experienced breeder is very important.

Because certain health issues exist in a breed, breeders may have knowledge that could mitigate the veterinarian's advice to neuter your show dog. I am not advising against a competent vet's recommendations; I am, however, suggesting that your vet have a discussion with an experienced breeder of your breed. It might help save your dog from being barred from showing and permanently unable to reproduce.

A Word on Nutrition

I've discussed this topic with owners and breeders of top-winning show dogs of all breeds and all sizes and hailing from all parts of the world. These conversations have drawn me to one conclusion: what works well varies as widely as the breeds and individual dogs within those breeds.

Your breeder should be aware of health conditions that exist in your breed.

If there is an answer at all to the question of proper feeding, it is probably to feed what works best. What's best is not necessarily what your dog likes best, but it will most likely keep your dog looking and behaving in competitive shape.

Let's not forget we're talking about competitive animals here. When your pooch is competing with top-class dogs of his or her breed, being in just "good" shape is not going to cut it. A dog is in top condition or it's not—it's all or nothing. Muscle tone, coat quality, and attitude all rely heavily on proper nutrition.

Good nutrition will show itself in your dog's shiny coat and overall healthy form.

Who can tell you just what kind of food to feed your dog? I recommend you consult the breeder from

Part 1

Treats are good training motivators, but make sure they are nutritious.

Choose a good-quality dog food that is formulated for your dog's stage of life.

whom you purchased your show dog or your foundation stock. I can only assume you began with the breeder you selected because of the outstanding dogs bred there and the show records those dogs acquired. Whatever your breeder has been doing works for the dogs he or she is breeding.

The amount of food your dog should be given depends upon the amount of exercise your dog is getting and how he uses up the calories consumed. A Border Collie working sheep all day long needs considerably more food than a geriatric Basset Hound whose exercise is limited to a daily leisurely walk around the block.

If there were a rule of thumb, I would say the correct amount of food for a normally active dog of any breed is the amount the dog will eat readily within about 15 minutes of being given the meal. What your dog does not eat in that length of time should be taken up and discarded. Leaving food out for extended periods of time can lead to erratic and finicky eating habits.

Chow Hounds

Whether canned or dry, look for a food in which the main ingredient is derived from meat, poultry, or fish. Arguments are often presented that dogs are not really carnivores but actually vegetarians. However, no wild canine I've ever heard of has gone out to slaughter a row of corn or bring home a bushel of potatoes for those hungry pups.

The canine world dines on animal protein. Granted, the animals they consume sustain themselves on plant life, but they've processed their intake into flesh, and that is what our canine friends are after. Manufacturers of quality dog foods are aware of this process and develop their products accordingly.

Be aware that a top-quality dog food is pricier than lower-quality dog food. In many cases, you will find your dog not only needs less of the better food, but there will also be less fecal matter to clean up as well.

Safe chew toys can keep your dog occupied and his teeth healthy.

Dog foods advertised and packaged to look like a steak, a ham bone, or blocks of cheese are prepared that way to appeal to the dog owner, not the dog. Your dog doesn't give two hoots that something looks like a juicy steak or a wedge of cheddar cheese. All he cares about is how what you're offering smells and tastes. The "looks-like" dog foods are manufactured that way to tempt you. Unless you plan to join your dog for dinner, don't waste your money.

You can tell whether or not your dog is receiving the proper amount of food by closely monitoring the dog's condition. You should be able to feel the ribs and backbone through a slight layer of muscle and fat. Again, good judgment should prevail. Don't expect your thin-skinned Whippet to feel like the neighbor's heavy-bodied and well-fleshed Chow.

Nylabone® makes edible treats for your dog.

Fresh water and a properly prepared, balanced diet containing all the essential nutrients in correct proportions is all a healthy dog should be offered. If your dog doesn't want to eat the food offered, it's

Food Dyes

Be careful of those canned or moist products that are advertised as having the look of "lean red beef," or the dry foods that are red in color. This is especially important if you have a long-haired, white, or light-colored dog. Usually, the color is put there to appeal to you, and it looks that way through the use of red dye. Those dyes will invariably stain the hair around the light-colored dogs' face—often permanently or until you stop using the product and the hair completely grows out.

A good red-dye test is to place a small amount of the canned or dry food that you have moistened well on a piece of white paper towel. Let the food sit there for a half-hour or so and then check to see if there is any red staining on the towel. If the toweling has taken on a red stain, you can rest assured that before too long a time your dog's whiskers will be the same color.

All dogs need grooming to keep their coats in maximum condition.

because he is either not hungry or not feeling well. If the former is the case, Rover will eat when he is hungry.

If, on the other hand, you find lack of appetite is affecting your dog's condition, you have good reason to suspect your dog is not well. When this is the case, an appointment with your veterinarian is definitely in order.

There are so many excellent commercial dog foods available today that make it very easy to choose one of these carefully thought-out products. It is important, however, that you read packaging labels carefully or consult with your veterinarian, who will assist you in selecting the best moist or dry food for your dog.

Grooming

Just as all dogs must be kept at the peak of health, well conditioned, and fed properly to achieve their potential as show dogs, they must also be groomed. Understand one thing clearly—all breeds of dogs must be regularly groomed to keep their coats in top shape. This applies tenfold to show dogs, whether we're talking sleek-coated Dobermans or long-haired and exotically trimmed Poodles.

No judge will let you get by with a dirty dog or one whose coat is matted and tangled. Nor will the judge be impressed with a smooth-coated dog whose coat is dull and lifeless. So, if you are trying to make your choice of breeds on the basis of zero grooming, think again. You'd think a satin-smooth Whippet or Miniature Pinscher wouldn't take any more than a lick and a promise to get ready for the ring–right? Unfortunately, this is not the case.

Just walk back into the grooming area of a dog show before judging times for those breeds and watch the exhibitors getting their dogs ready. Talk to the exhibitors about the preparation that takes place weeks and months before show time. Granted, there are breeds that require *less* work than others, but there are no breeds that require none. There are also all those breeds that not only require good coat care, but also intricate and detailed work with scissors or by hand before they can be presented in the ring.

Some dogs, like the Poodle, need extensive grooming for the show ring.

The accompanying list includes the relatively popular breeds that require rather extensive preparation before they can be shown on a competitive basis. This is not to say that they are the only breeds requiring extensive grooming. You need only attend a few shows before it becomes apparent that some exhibitors have gotten the hang of how to get their breed ready for the ring and some have not.

There are some breeds, such as Poodles and Löwchen, that are subject to disqualification by the judge unless they are clipped to a certain specific pattern. Other breeds, like the Cavalier King Charles Spaniel and the Havanese, incur penalties if the coat is clipped or trimmed.

Grooming Needs

Grooming these breeds require special training to achieve the proper effect for show dogs.

Cocker Spaniel	Kerry Blue Terrier	Shih Tzu
English Cocker Spaniel	Lakeland Terrier	Yorkshire Terrier
English Setter	Miniature Schnauzer	Bichon Frise
English Springer Spaniel	Norfolk Terrier	Chow Chow
Golden Retriever	Norwich Terrier	Keeshond
Gordon Setter	Scottish Terrier	Lhasa Apso
Irish Setter	Sealyham Terrier	Löwchen
Irish Water Spaniel	Skye Terrier	Poodle
Airedale Terrier	Soft Coated Wheaten Terrier	Bearded Collie
Australian Terrier	Welsh Terrier	Bouvier des Flandres
Bedlington Terrier	West Highland White Terrier	Briard
Border Terrier	Affenpinscher	Collie
Cairn Terrier	Brussels Griffon	Old English Sheepdog
Dandie Dinmont Terrier	Maltese	Puli
Wire Fox Terrier	Pekingese	Shetland Sheepdog
Irish Terrier	Pomeranian	

All the "broken-coated" terriers like Airedale, Wire Fox, and Norfolk Terriers require hand removal or plucking of the hair in defined, graduated steps so that the new coat grows in, with not only proper texture, but also in the proper length for a given time or show date. There are other terriers like the Soft Coated Wheaten, Bedlington, and Kerry Blue that require extensive scissor work. There can be no doubt that "putting down" a terrier is an art that takes years of practice to perfect. Whether amateur or professional, those who excel in doing so are held in high regard by their peers.

A broken coat consists of a harsh and often wiry outer jacket, plus a dense softer undercoat. In overall texture, it resembles coconut matting. When it attains maximum length, the outer coat tends to soften or "blow." For all intents and purposes it is "dead" hair that is relatively loose and easily removed with minimal discomfort to the dog.

Hair Growing "Miracles"

I'm sure you've seen all those television commercials claiming the new wonder product is guaranteed to grow hair on a billiard ball or some such. Ever since I began raising show dogs, there have been similar claims made for miracle products that applied topically or ingested will grow a coat on a Bulldog that will put Old English Sheepdogs to shame. These "too-good-to-be-true" products are exactly that—too good to be true.

There is nothing—and I repeat—absolutely nothing that will make a dog's coat grow where the dog's genetic makeup didn't intend for the hair to grow, nor will the product make the coat grow beyond the amount its genotype permits.

Bea Weguson, a great breeder of Cocker Spaniels back in the 60s, was often asked what she did and what she fed to give her dogs the heavy coats they always carried. She always replied, "It's an ancient recipe handed down to me from my great grandmother—one part good clean food and two parts elbow grease with a good brush."

Terriers may need to have their coats stripped or plucked on a regular basis.

Good grooming will keep your dog looking and feeling fine.

Words from the Wise

Lydia Coleman Hutchinson
Wolfpit Cairn Terriers

In the highly competitive world of terriers, there is no argument that the professional holds court more often than not. However, there are those within terrierdom whose staunch loyalty to their respective breeds and their determination to succeed has maintained a place for the owner-handler. Lydia Coleman Hutchinson of Middletown, Maryland is one of those people.

She has shown dogs for over 50 years, and over those years has bred approximately 160 champions. Lydia estimates that about half of them were bred with her parents, Esther and Taylor Coleman–a family affair indeed. She calculates that she has shown over 100 of these champions to their titles. A good many of the others bred at Wolfpit were sold to other breeders and exhibitors who handled the dogs to their championships themselves.

The Wolfpit Cairn Terrier Clan: Esther Cotman with Ch. Bonnie Scamp of Wolfpit, (left); Esther's daughter, Lydia Coleman Hutchinson, with Scamp's daughter, Ch. Bonnie Vixen of Wolfpit (right); and Lydia's daughter, Susan Taylor Hutchinson, with Vixen's daughter, Ch. Bonnie Vamp of Wolfpit (center).

In a Variety Group that calls upon the epitome of grooming and presentation, the less "prepared" dogs are often left from the spotlight. This was not to be the case as far as Lydia and her ruggedly natural Cairns were concerned. She has handled the Wolfpit Cairn Terriers to six All-Breed Bests in Show and over 30 Terrier Group Firsts. Among the other Wolfpit accomplishments are the numerous Bests of Breed, Bests of Opposite Sex, Awards of Merit, and point wins at National Specialties.

Lydia has said, "What I am most pleased with is not the show records our dogs have amassed but their producing records. Wolfpit has owned four of the top-producing sires in Cairns, including the all-time top producer Ch. Cairnwood's Quince, and at least 10 top producing dams. Our bloodlines can be found throughout the US and somewhat in Canada."

The sincerity in Lydia Coleman Hutchinson's advice to those who wish to succeed in doing justice to their own dogs are best captured in her own words.

"I was so young and innocent when I got involved in the wonderful world of purebred dogs that I didn't realize how it would envelop my life and that of my family. In retrospect, I would like to have taken some animal husbandry and canine anatomy courses in college, but if I'd chosen a college where those were offered, I never would have met my marvelous husband who has been so supportive of my 'dog addiction' over the past 42-plus years.

"I wish I'd known of the heartbreaks that can come with breeding and showing your own dogs. Unless you've personally experienced those sad times, you cannot truly understand the depths of emotion involved. But there are many times when the joy of being involved in such a hard endeavor makes up for the heartbreaks.

"I had such good teachers from the first time I showed at age ten that I was able to hone my natural abilities quite easily. I was able to build rapport with the dogs I trained from early on, which, I suppose, is what Miss Ruelle Kelchner of Hollycourt Miniature Poodles saw in me when I was just 13 years old and asked me to show-train all the puppies in her large kennel. I worked for her during most of my teen years."

Socializing and Training Your Show Dog

There is one lesson that all dogs—show dogs or not—must learn. They must learn to get along well with people and behave sensibly around other dogs. It's certain that no dog should go anywhere near a dog show if he cannot be fully trusted.

Dog show judges are people who love dogs. If they didn't, they wouldn't be doing what they do. However, no person, no matter how much they may love dogs, wants to be bitten by one. It goes without saying that other exhibitors and spectators don't have a burning desire to have your dog brutalize them or their dogs.

Dogs that are not accustomed to being handled

Dogs that compete in dog shows should be well socialized.

Part 1

Your show dog must get used to being handled by strangers.

Biting Dogs

When a dog is disqualified for attacking either a person or another dog in the ring, any awards that the offending dog wins at that event will be canceled by the AKC. The dog won't be able to compete again unless, following application by the owner to the AKC, the owner has received official notification from the AKC that the dog's event eligibility has been reinstated, in accordance with the Rules Applying to Dog Shows, Obedience Regulations, or Regulations for Agility Trials.

by strangers, particularly those breeds with a wary or protective nature, can easily overreact to being touched by people they do not know. A frightened or nervous dog will invariably act in one of two ways—either by shrinking away and attempting to escape or by biting in self-defense. I assure you that neither recourse will enhance the dog's image in the eyes of the judge. If your dog will not stand to be examined, he will be excused from the class. Attempting to bite or actually biting will get your dog barred from competition. Chronic offenders could be barred from competition for the rest of their lives.

This doesn't mean your dog has to lavish affection on every person that comes along. In some breeds, a wary attitude or an aloof nature is a natural part of breed character. However, all show dogs must stand for examination, and there is no tolerance for those that won't.

Sound temperament is what enables a dog to calmly accept being handled by strangers. Good temperament is inherited but can also be enhanced by socialization. Poor treatment and lack of socialization can ruin a dog's inherited good temperament. A dog that has inherited a bad temperament is, at best, a nuisance and, at worst, downright dangerous. A dog with a bad temperament has no place in the average home, much less in the show ring.

Even dogs trained for personal protection are taught to stand and be touched by a stranger if their owner gives the command. No dog, regardless of origin and purpose or what the dog may be trained to do, should ever arbitrarily attempt to attack anyone or anything.

Lessons to Learn

Sharon Newcomb of Santa Fe, New Mexico takes "Luke," her 150-pound Anatolian Shepherd, to neighborhood schools to give the children a demonstration on how they should and should not approach a strange dog. Anatolian Shepherds are an ancient breed developed to protect livestock throughout the Middle East.

In many cases, the flocks they guard in their homeland represent the sum total of the family's worldly goods. Therefore, the dogs must protect their charges at all costs. An Anatolian would lay down his own life in defense of literally anything he has been put in charge of—animal, human, or property. The dogs are big enough and tough enough to easily dispatch a wolf or human if necessary.

Good temperament is both inherited and learned.

Sharon begins her lesson by making it clear that no one, especially children, should ever touch a dog they do not know without asking permission of the owner. Then she has the children come and pet Luke. The children just naturally love the big dog and do most anything to show their feelings, including hugging him around the neck and kissing him on the nose. Luke patiently endures it all.

Sharon then invites one of the teachers to do the same, and Luke accepts attention from the adult as well. She then puts Luke on a leash and gives the "watch" command. She then has the teacher hold a yardstick in hand and approach them in a menacing manner. In an instant, Luke transforms himself from a calm and enduring "good old boy" to a snarling beast, teeth bared, ready to defend his mistress at all costs.

Children should be taught the proper way to behave around dogs.

A good breeder will start a puppy's socialization process right away.

The demonstration is really done to show the children that looks can be deceiving, and that no one knows what a strange dog is capable of doing. At the same time, it demonstrates how even dogs of the most protective natures can and should be trained to behave like good citizens.

There is no doubt that the noise and the tense competitive atmosphere of dog shows sends stress levels soaring in both humans and dogs that are unaccustomed to it. What most new exhibitors do not realize is that their dogs are extremely sensitive to their owners' moods and anxiety levels. When a new and nervous owner becomes anxious, that message is transmitted right down the leash to the dog. The dog goes on high alert.

A well-socialized dog with a sound temperament can be introduced to the unending complications and stresses of modern living, including those found at dog shows, and survive. Responsible breeders do everything in their power to produce stable temperaments in their bloodlines. If you never take your dog outside your front door from the day you purchase him until the two of you are off to your first dog show, don't blame the dog for reacting with fear—blame yourself.

A part of a good breeder's daily program is to give each puppy he or she raises personal attention and exposure to different situations. This kind of socialization must continue into adulthood. Understand that your dog may be happy and calm at home and in the backyard. However, if the socialization that began in puppyhood is not continued, that sunny disposition and extroverted showmanship will close down the minute you leave your home.

Curbing Aggression

Never encourage your puppy's aggressive behavior, even if he was purchased with the breed's guarding ability in mind. The protective instinct develops on its own as the dog approaches maturity, and it doesn't need to be stimulated by antagonizing the dog or by allowing aggressive behavior to arbitrarily manifest itself.

Growling and puppy bites on your hand may seem cute at eight weeks of age, but they are not so cute coming from a 100-pound dog, especially when he decides that he doesn't want to do what you want him to. If you don't like this behavior, you can imagine how strangers feel, having no idea whether that growling means he's ready to bite their head off or is just his way of "playing."

Nor should there be any reason for the pup to fear strangers. Once you leave the confines of your home, everything you do will be an adventure for the puppy and even for a new, adult dog. Your dog is going to be examined at every single dog show the two of you attend, so he might as well get accustomed to this examination from puppyhood.

You should teach your dog to greet strangers on the street with a friendly attitude, but also with restraint. You don't want your show dog to recoil in fear when any stranger approaches him, whether that stranger is a passerby or the judge in the ring. On the other hand, you won't want him to fling himself into a judge's arms with rapturous kisses when it's time for the examination.

Your puppy's aggressive behavior should never be encouraged.

Give your puppy plenty of Nylabones® when he is teething to control his biting and chewing.

At some point, most puppies will try to challenge your authority.

Show dogs must learn to get along with other dogs, especially in the ring.

Always remember that other dogs have just as much right to be at the dog show as yours. Your dog will have to get used to that fact. You may never be able to teach him to love the other dogs around him, but he must learn to tolerate them. This may not be the easiest thing in the world to teach males of some breeds–particularly the ones who are used for breeding. However, it is still your responsibility to keep your dog on a short leash and your attention focused on him every minute you are at the show. There is nothing more irritating for someone who has gone through all the effort of training his or her dog to behave well than to have that dog harassed by an out-of-control bully wandering through the aisles of a show on a long leash.

Dogs of some breeds, even those breeds of the mildest nature, can hit a point in their adolescence where they feel duty-bound to challenge you. For instance, when she was about five to six months old, one Corgi that I owned decided she would just see if a little growling would dissuade the judge from opening her mouth during the examination. The first time it happened, I was completely taken back, because the bitch I was showing was normally a real tail-wagger (well, perhaps a real stump-wagger).

The judge officiating that day was a Corgi breeder who had obviously been through this same scenario before. He took the dog by the shoulders, gave her a firm shake, and said, "No!" in such a commanding tone of voice that my pup blinked in surprise and never tried that little trick again. I've had others over the years that have attempted the same trick, but it has been me that let them know in no uncertain terms that this was not going to happen again–and it didn't.

Socialization

To assist your dog in socialization, he should go everywhere with you—the post office, along busy streets, the shopping mall. This applies to puppies as well as young adults. Carry treats with you when you go out. If your puppy backs off from a stranger, give the person one of the little snacks and have him or her offer it to your puppy. Insist that your young dog be amenable to the attention of any strangers you approve of, regardless of sex, age, or race.

Positive training will keep your dog's spirits up but his behavior in hand.

Males are going to have to get used to the fact that a required part of the judge's examination is checking the dog's testicles to make sure they are present and normally formed. This is a sensitive area for many males, so be sure to accustom him to this part of the examination.

Many young dogs are perfect ladies and gentleman out in public and wouldn't think of misbehaving or ignoring your commands. However, once they get to their first dog show, you'd think their brains have come loose from their heads. It's as if they've never had a lesson in their lives. That's simply because they are not accustomed to all those strange and wonderful sights and smells and all those dogs of so many shapes and sizes.

You've got to be able to get your dog under control, but not in a manner that's going to have him associate dog shows with punishment. The last thing you want is a dog with a bubbling personality to turn into a wilted rose as you enter the gates of the dog show. Training is important, but it has to be done properly. You should keep your dog's spirits up, but his behavior in hand.

Dog Show Etiquette

- Know exactly where you are going before you leave home so that you are not late for your ring call.

- Exercise your dog upon arrival at the show and shortly before ring time so that he will not have to do so in the show ring.

- Keep an eye on your dog all times, and, if you must be away from your dog, make sure he is securely crated or under the supervision of someone you know and trust.

- Do not let your dog wander at the end of your leash. All dogs are not as trustworthy as your own.

- Make sure you and your dog are clean, neat, and appropriately dressed.

- Be at ringside well ahead of time.

- Pay attention to the procedure followed by the judge and follow any directions he or she may give. Most judges use the same procedure throughout the day, and your paying attention will relieve the judge of having to give the same instructions all over again.

- Make sure your armband is securely located on your left arm and is clearly visible.

- Keep your dog between you and the judge at all times while you are in the ring.

- When you move your dog, keep a reasonable distance behind the dog ahead of you so that yours does not "run up" on another dog.

- Always congratulate the winner.

- Accept losses gracefully.

- Accept wins gracefully.

- *Never* use facial expressions to indicate you disagree with *anything* a judge may decide.

- Do not call a well-known dog by its name when a judge can hear you.

- Never snatch a ribbon from the judge's hand or use sarcastic tone of voice.

- Never physically reprimand your dog in the ring or on the show grounds.

- Do not follow a judge who has indicated he or she likes your dog from show to show.

Your dog will have to learn dog show etiquette, and the only place he can learn this is at a dog show. I'm sure you'll understand why waiting to begin those lessons until the two of you are at a major dog show may not be the wisest decision to make, so we'll look at alternative methods to teach your dog to put his best foot forward when he enters the show grounds.

Training

Any dog you bring into your home has a great deal to learn so that he can fit into the lifestyle of your household. There's a whole other set of behaviors your dog will have to learn in order to fit comfortably into the life of a show dog.

You are fortunate if your future show star came to you at an early stage of life. The two of you can work into all the dog show lessons slowly. It's so much easier to get your message across to a puppy than it is to a fully matured adult that is set in his ways.

Crate Training

A major key to successfully training your dog for anything–whether it's obedience training, house-training, or becoming a show dog–is a dog crate. First-time dog owners are inclined to initially see the use of a crate or cage as cruel. However, those same people–even the ones who bought their dog simply as a companion–have returned later to thank me profusely for having suggested using a crate for their new acquisition. New owners are also surprised to find their puppy will eventually come to think of his crate as a place of private retreat, a den to which he can go for rest and privacy.

Crate training is important for your show dog, as he will spend a lot of time there.

Use of a crate reduces housetraining time down to an absolute minimum and avoids keeping a puppy under constant stress by incessantly correcting him for making mistakes in the

The Nylabone® Fold Away Pet Carrier folds for easy storage.

Give your pup a toy or a Nylabone® to keep him happy in his crate.

house. The crate gives you a safe place to put your dog when you are not there to supervise what he is doing. As far as show people are concerned, a crate is as important as a collar, leash, and brush. It is a bottom-line necessity.

Show dogs spend a lot of time going to and coming from shows and other places. When they travel in their own crate, they are never in entirely strange surroundings. The crate with a soft blanket at its bottom is a familiar piece of home, offering the puppy or dog security no matter where he may go. Even in your car, traveling in a secured crate precludes the possibility of your dog being injured or killed by being thrown against a window in a sudden stop.

Airlines will accept shipping your dog as excess baggage in no other way than in a crate. Even the tiny breeds that can fit under the seat in front of you must travel in a mini-crate or at least a soft carrier or bag, or they will not be allowed to board the plane. At shows, a crate is the only safe place your dog can be other than standing right beside you with a leash held firmly in hand. Crates and cages come in a wide variety of styles and sizes to choose from. The Nylabone® Fold Away Pet Carrier is an excellent choice, because it folds for easier storage when not in use.

If your puppy is not already accustomed to a crate when he first arrives, begin using it as the place where he has his meals. Keep the door closed and latched while he's eating. When he's finished, open the cage and carry him outdoors to the spot where you want him to learn to eliminate. If you consistently take your puppy to the same spot, you will reinforce the habit of going there for that purpose.

Initially, put the puppy into the crate for short periods of time when you can be in the same room. Every time you put him in the crate, give him a small treat of some kind. Throw the treat to the back of the crate and encourage the puppy to walk in on his own. When he does so, praise him, and perhaps hand him another piece of the treat through the opening in the front of the crate or put a toy or a Nylabone® in that will get his attention right away.

Do not succumb to his complaints about being in his crate. Your puppy must learn to stay there and without unnecessary complaining. Ignoring the dog if he fusses will usually get the puppy to understand theatrics will not result in liberation. Only let him out when he is being quiet, or he'll get the wrong message.

Understand that an 8- to 12-week-old puppy will not be able to contain himself for long periods of time. Puppies of that age must relieve themselves every few hours, except at night. Adjust your schedule accordingly. Also, make sure that your puppy has relieved himself the last thing at night and do not dawdle when you wake up in the morning.

Crate training is the best way to house-train your dog.

Your first priority in the morning is to get the puppy outdoors. Just how early this ritual will take place will depend much more upon your puppy's schedule than upon yours. If your dog is like most others, there will be no doubt in your mind when it needs to be let out. Very quickly, you'll also learn to tell the difference between the "this-is-an-emergency" complaint and the "I-just-want-out" grumbling.

Motion Sickness

It's highly unlikely that you'll find a dog show within walking distance of your home. Even if there were a show just down the road, you'll quickly become aware that, with most

It may take some time for your puppy to get used to car travel.

Make sure your dogs get plenty of exercise while on the road.

breeds, there will be more items to take to that show than you could possibly stuff into your backpack.

Therefore, your dog will have to become accustomed to riding in a car. With many dogs, riding in a car is a snap, and from their very first ride, the rattle of the car keys will have them at the door, tap dancing in anticipation. That doesn't apply to all dogs, however. There are just as many that experience motion sickness.

In most cases, short rides—no more than five minutes or so—once or twice a day will gradually accustom the dog to riding in the car, and the problem is over, never to return. There are other dogs, however, that have a terrible time with motion sickness, and even sitting in a motionless car will set them to drooling and emptying the contents of their stomachs.

This can develop into problems that can increase in intensity and duration if not dealt with properly. Obviously, no dog is going to be at his best when he arrives at a show with stomach in roaring upset and covered with drool from head to toes. It can take some dogs many hours to recuperate from the ill effects of carsickness.

Most dogs are easily treated through the use of a prescription drug administered a short time before the ride. This medicine can be obtained from your veterinarian, who is able to prescribe the proper dose for your breed of dog. More intense cases might require a tranquilizer to calm the dog's nerves and fears. Again, this is a drug that should be administered only under the supervision of your regular vet.

Real problem cases take both the use of mediation along with considerable time and a lot of patience. I have found the best way to accustom chronic cases of motion sickness is to have the dog associate the stationary car with treats and fun. First, don't feed the dog immediately before traveling to lessen the chances of stomach upset. Begin by throwing a treat or a toy into the open car and praising the dog profusely when he retrieves it.

Sitting in the car without the motor on for four or five minutes at a time and rewarding the dog with a treat is the next step. Extend the time bit by bit until he seems relatively comfortable sitting there. Do not turn on the motor until you are sure your dog is totally at ease.

Next step is to sit in the car with the motor running but standing still. Make the first ride no more than a block. Stop, get out of the car with the dog, and let him settle for a few minutes. Put him back into the car and go directly home.

Lavish praise and a treat of some kind should follow this process. Gradually increase the distance you travel, but the minute you observe dizziness or drooling, stop and get the dog out of the car.

Use a crate, like the Nylabone® Fold Away Pet Carrier, to keep the dog safely restrained. Keep calm and keep reassuring the dog. Do everything in small increments, and eventually you will be on your way to happier days and longer road trips.

Table Manners

Most of the smaller and many of the medium-sized breeds are placed on the judges' table at dog shows in order to be examined by the judge. The judges' table is exactly the same kind most exhibitors use to groom their dogs. Although the larger breeds are not examined on a table, most exhibitors place their dogs on them to groom and prepare them for the ring.

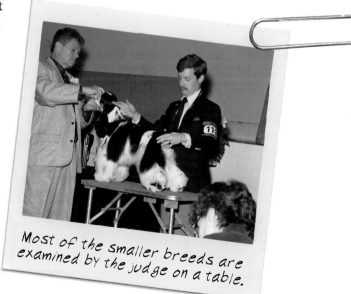

Most of the smaller breeds are examined by the judge on a table.

Part 1

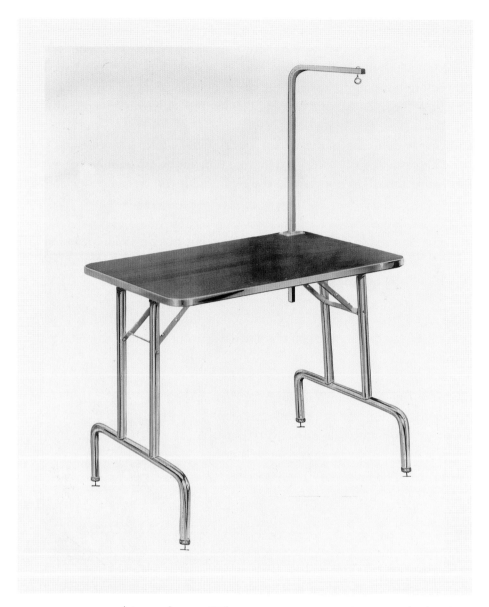

Grooming table with arm. The arm is an excellent method of keeping the dog from moving around during grooming; however, the dog should never be attached to a grooming arm if no one is present.

Regardless of whether your dog is a table breed or not, it's a whole lot easier getting those rubber band legs of a pup all going in same direction when you can pull him together on a table rather than scrambling around on the floor.

Therefore, beginning your initial training on one of these grooming tables works in your favor, regardless of your pup's potential size. You won't be hoisting any of the giant breeds up on a table for very long, but we'll get to the big guys shortly.

The table you select should be sturdy and covered with a non-slip rubber top. There are all kinds of grooming tables: Some are portable and have telescoping legs that also fold up flat against the bottom of the table and can be easily transported; others are an integral part of the crate in which your dog will travel to the show. Time and experience will lead you to the correct table for your breed.

The table is where you can begin your posing or, in the dog show vernacular, "stacking" lessons. This simply means you will learn to set your dog up so that he conforms best to the stance described in your breed standard. Looking through pictures of books and magazines at photos of your breed, you will note that attempts are made to conform to a certain "look."

Note how the head is positioned, how the legs are placed, the level of the back, and where the handler's hands are placed. Learning to do this quickly and to your dog's best advantage is extremely important,

Select a sturdy table with a non-slip rubber top.

Learning to stack your dog properly takes time and practice.

Part 1

When stacking your dog, present him to his best advantage.

"Stacking" Your Dog

The judge asks the exhibitor to "stack" or pose his or her dog so that the dog is presented in the best position possible to access his quality. Whether your breed of dog is posed in line with the other dogs or alone for examination on the ground or on a table, it is always done with the dog faced in a counter-clockwise direction. Therefore you must practice posing your dog from its right side. This gives your right hand freedom to control the dog's head and your left hand to set the legs in proper position.

because invariably it will be the first thing that the officiating judge will ask you to do once you enter the ring. There's a tried and true saying among dog folk that you should never forget: "You don't get a second chance to make a first impression."

The judge will have you stack your dog again when he or she is ready to begin the examination. Remember that the judge doesn't have all afternoon for you to get your dog in position, and posing your dog poorly can create faults that are not really there. On the other hand, setting a dog up cleverly can help disguise shortcomings that your dog may have.

Yes, the judge should be able to discover these flaws if the faults are really there, but note that I say "should be able." If the judge does not find them, that's his or her problem. All dogs have faults of one kind or another. There's no need for you to point them out. You are there to win, and presenting your dog in the best possible light to make this happen is your primary concern.

Sometimes it takes a bit of a tug here or a lift there, but eventually you will begin to see that your dog can look 100-percent better when properly posed. Simply plunking him down with legs and feet pointing in all directions will not do.

Doing this gently and repeatedly in very short sessions can begin even with five- to six-week-old puppies, so that by the time your pup is fully grown, posing properly is old hat. Be extremely careful at all times to avoid having your pup jump off the table. Serious and permanent injuries, even death, can occur if this happens.

Realize that you are dealing with a baby, and attention spans are extremely brief at a young age. Never make dog show lessons drudgery or allow your dog to associate dog shows with punishment. Doing so may destroy his desire to be there at all, and you may never be able to restore the sparkling attitude that helps put the dog in first place.

Getting your dog accustomed to the table will make grooming chores a whole lot easier as well. He'll understand that the table means business, and whether it's posing or being brushed, there's work to be done.

After my dogs are accustomed to standing on the table, I like to teach them to lie down on it as well. This is especially important with coated dogs, because it allows you to get at all the difficult to reach places with your brush. Mats accumulate in the dog's "armpits" and around the dog's genitals–difficult places to brush out thoroughly with the dog standing. They can be easier to work on with the dog lying on his side.

Through the Looking Glass

The best way I know of learning how to get your dog set up properly is to place a large-sized mirror on the wall and learn to pose your dog by seeing what you accomplish while you're doing it. At shows, you can't tell what the judge might be seeing as he or she stands in the middle of the ring. However, if you practice posing your dog to duplicate the pictures of the winning dogs in the publications, all the while watching yourself in the mirror, you will begin to learn what you have to do get the desired stacking pose.

The judge will ask you to stack your dog when he is ready to examine him.

Get your puppy accustomed to the table when he is young.

Grooming Table Danger

Grooming tables are very important and useful aids at home and at dog shows. They can also be very hazardous. Never leave your dog unattended on a grooming table. You can never be entirely sure that some passing dog might not entice him to jump down and run off. In the case of the smaller dogs, broken legs can be just the least of sustained injuries. Many tables come equipped with grooming "arms," a vertical bar that fixes onto the table with an angle at the top to which a fastener is attached to the dog's collar. This is an excellent precaution to use if you are present. It keeps the dog standing in place while you are grooming. However, if you are not there and the dog attempts to jump down, he can strangle himself. If you or someone responsible cannot be present, put your dog in a crate until you return.

It is easier to groom a dog that is used to a grooming table.

Teaching some dogs to lie down on the table can be a bit of a chore at first, but once a dog gets accustomed to it, he will become entirely comfortable and will probably take a snooze while his owners do all the hard work. Training your dog to lie comfortably on a grooming table is best started when he is a puppy, but even an adult dog will respond well if you are firm and gentle. Begin by picking your dog up as you

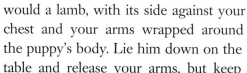

No Mats!

Speaking as a judge, there is nothing I find more irritating in examining coated breeds than finding mats in the coat. As far as I'm concerned, it shows neglect and slip-shod presentation. Obviously, the exhibitor doesn't feel his or her dog warrants the care due to a winner. If the exhibitor doesn't feel the dog should be classed as a winner, why should I? This could be the difference between winning a award or going home disappointed.

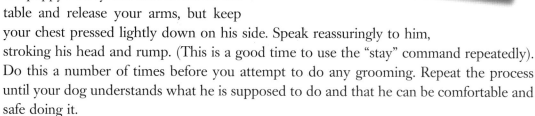

Make the grooming table a pleasant experience for your dog with treats and praise.

would a lamb, with its side against your chest and your arms wrapped around the puppy's body. Lie him down on the table and release your arms, but keep your chest pressed lightly down on his side. Speak reassuringly to him, stroking his head and rump. (This is a good time to use the "stay" command repeatedly). Do this a number of times before you attempt to do any grooming. Repeat the process until your dog understands what he is supposed to do and that he can be comfortable and safe doing it.

Free Stacking and Baiting

A good number of the breeds are posed on the table for examination, but every breed is observed by the judge when they are down on the ground. The handlers of some of the table breeds kneel down on the ground and stack their dogs by hand as they would on the table.

There are, however, a good many breeds, particularly the larger ones, that are customarily shown either posed on the ground or standing on their own, without the handler

Although many breeds are examined on tables, they are also posed and observed on the ground. Don Johnson poses the author's Cocker Spaniel, Ch. Beau Monde More Paint.

Barbara Powers similarly poses her longhaired Dachshund, Ch.
Bermarg's Stony of Boondox L.

No matter how cute he is, your dog should stand alert when in front of a judge.

physically putting the dog into position. Many judges will insist upon seeing even the hand-posed breeds stand on their own at some point during the judging. This requires training your dog to stand on command, in its own natural position with its four legs in place, and head and tail in the correct position for your particular breed. All this should take place without any contact assistance from you. This is called free stacking.

Naturally, you don't want your dog to stand there like a limp dishrag–you want him to be a picture of alertness and vigor. The desired effect is a stance that shows off his best attributes. The best way to get your dog's attention and have him stand there looking the part is through the use of what is referred to as bait–a small piece of food that the dog really likes. Yes, it's the same kind of baiting technique the fisherman employs, only in this case the bait will be used to get and hold your dog's attention rather than hook and reel him in. The best kind of bait to use is obviously the kind your dog likes best.

Most experienced handlers use freshly cooked liver that's often available for sale at the dog shows booths. However, I know some dogs who wouldn't give two sniffs at a piece of liver, but would stand on their tiptoes for the rest of the day for a piece of hot dog or chunk of chicken breast. What's best for your dog? Whatever works.

Practice Makes Perfect

Observe the successful people in your breed to learn how to set up your dog to his best advantage. Long-time owner-handlers and professional handlers employ certain techniques they've learned over the years that show your breed off best. Try to emulate what they do and, as I suggested, practice in front of a mirror.

However, it stands to reason that you can look in a mirror, but if you aren't aware of the mistakes you are making, you'll never be able to correct them. Many breed and all-breed clubs hold regularly scheduled handling classes where beginners can take their dogs to learn how to show them. The classes are usually run by experienced professional handlers who volunteer their time or by amateurs who have developed great skill in presenting their own dogs and who enjoy assisting others in learning to do the same thing.

This is also where you will learn to gait your dog in the proper manner and at the proper speed. Judges have different ways in which they like to observe dogs being gaited in their rings. Later chapters will give you greater detail on those patterns of movement.

The classes help by critiquing your handling technique, as well as teaching your dog what to do in the show ring. Your dog will also learn that he has to do what you want him to, despite the fact that there are all kinds of strange dogs around who look like they'd be tons of fun to romp with.

Handling class is very similar to what you and your dog will encounter at every dog show you attend, and you'll have to work as a team despite what is going on around you. Your dog will make mistakes in class and so will you, but you'll have people there to help you correct them and these classroom errors won't cost you a win.

Practice makes perfect–repetition helps when learning to stack your dog properly.

Handling classes can help you become familiar with showing techniques and procedures.

Part 1

Words from the Wise

Leon Goetz
Reverie Australian Shepherds

Leon Goetz, the Dallas, Texas Australian Shepherd breeder and owner-handler has been showing dogs for 13 years, a relatively short time compared to many of our successful owner-handlers. He proves, however, that getting to the top is obviously more than just a matter of time. Once he got started, it was straight up in the win department. He's racked up 14 All-Breed Bests in Show, 70 Group Firsts, and 2 Bests in Show at the Aussie National Specialty with two different dogs in two consecutive years.

Leon Goetz pictured with one of his top-winning Australian Shepherds.

When I asked Leon what knowledge he could have had in the beginning that might have put him on the winning track more quickly, he said, "The truth of the matter is that, for me, ignorance was truly bliss. I guess if I had realized how time consuming and how much effort this dog game required, I would have been discouraged from the onset. However, when we do not realize what is ahead, I think we sort of plod along, advancing one step at a time. It has been true in building my small business, and it is true for my efforts in the dog world.

"There's a saying in Texas: 'I wasn't born here, but I got here as fast as I could!' As a native Arkansan, the saying is also true for me in the sport of dogs. My first love was showing horses, so I didn't get started with dogs until my early 30s. While I have bred and owned a handful of Champions, my real interest was showing a special for the breed and group rings."

Leon continues: "When I acquired the future Ch. Silverwood's Texas Justice, I had naive hopes of making him a top special. The fact that it turned out that way, against all odds, is pretty unbelievable to me even today. I had people tell me to give up on him, that he would never make a special.

My refusal to do so resulted in his being the Number 7 Herding Dog in 2000 and the Number 2 top-winning Australian Shepherd and top-winning owner-handled Aussie in breed history.

"In addition, he won the breed at the Westminster Kennel Club show in New York twice and became the first and only Australian Shepherd (to date) to place in the Herding Group there. I retired him shortly after by winning the National Specialty in 2001.

 "My point in relaying all of this is that I always had goals in mind. There were things I wanted to achieve and while it wasn't always easy, there was enough success involved to keep me going–even when I was most discouraged and ready to give up.

"I truly believe that if an owner-handler has beautiful dogs and does their homework, success is attainable. As an owner-handler, I am constantly trying to learn and ultimately improve myself as well as my dogs. Setbacks make you stronger…never give up!

"Nothing in this sport comes easy…breeding, showing, performance…all require commitment. I read somewhere once that 'Perseverance will take you far.' I guess that has been somewhat of a guiding motto for me throughout all endeavors of my life. It certainly holds true in the sport of dogs if while hanging in there, you remember to work hard, learn every day, and above all, play fair!"

Traveling with Your Dog

If you're going to be serious about showing your dog, you are probably going to have to do some serious traveling. Travel involves advance planning, and the greater the distance you're going to travel, the more considerable the preparations you'll have to make. If there's air travel involved in your plans, there will be a number of advance reservations, weather checks, and legal requirements that must be met as well.

Serious showing will involve traveling with your dog.

Auto Travel

If your preferred means of transportation might have been a smart little sports car in the past, you can continue right on in that mode as long as your travel companion is a Chihuahua. But if your pal is anything bigger than a Cocker Spaniel, start

Part 1

Traveling with your dog requires thought and preparation.

The weather should be an important consideration before planning a trip.

rethinking how the two of you will survive a full day's journey crammed next to each other in the front of a sports car.

Don't forget that little puppies often grow into large dogs, and although your Great Dane pup snuggled into a bucket seat when he was six weeks old, he'll need his seat and yours at six months of age.

Forget about leaving your dog in the car by himself. Even on a mildly warm day, your St. Bernard will use up all of the available oxygen in a closed car at a rate that might surprise you. And temperatures can rise very quickly, making it downright dangerous to your pup's health, as well as illegal in many states.

Do think about available space and what you'll be transporting. Consider the safety of both your dog and your valuables. The larger the car, the easier it will be to safely accommodate your dog, yourself, and what you'll need to take with you. Station wagons, SUVs, and recreational vehicles are extremely popular and infinitely more useful for dog showing than a sports car or sedan.

Did you ever imagine that one day you would be buying a car for your dog? This is another item you'll need to add to all that nonexistent money that your friends will ask if you've won. There's no such thing as a bargain-priced show dog, no matter what you may have paid.

Time and Temperature

Two of the most important things to seriously consider before you embark on any kind of trip are temperatures

Part 1

(at home, along the way, and at your destination) and the length of time required for the stops you will be making on the road.

Most cars have air conditioning, and that will keep things at a comfortable temperature until you have to stop. Going a few miles down the road is one thing; a day's journey represents rest and food stops for both you and your dog.

Temperatures up to about 80°F are certainly bearable and shouldn't cause great concern to any but the very short-nosed breeds. However, leaving windows open really doesn't help much on a hot day, and the sun shining through the front and rear windows will send temperatures up and the metal of the vehicle seems to trap the

Some dogs love the car and will happily accompany you.

heat inside. If your dog is safely confined in his crate or cage, it will be just that much warmer. On a sunny day, the temperature inside a parked car, even a car with the window rolled down partway, can soar up 20 or 30 degrees in a matter of minutes. No dog is able to sustain these temperatures without suffering permanent brain damage or death. Do not take chances with your dog in a car on warm days.

You will have to plan stops along the way, whether it's winter or summer. Will your dog be able to accompany you indoors or to a shaded spot? Most restaurants in the US will not permit you to take your dog inside, no matter what the weather is like. You may find that those fine gourmet restaurants you are accustomed to dining in will have to be put on the save-for-later list. Drive-through meals or picnics under a shady tree along the road will become standard fare.

Safety First

Buckle up for safety—that applies to both you and Rover. Canine seat belts are now available and can be adapted to most any make of car and size of dog. This provides both the safety and restraint that can ensure both you and your dog a comfortable and safe trip.

The Nylabone® Fold Away Pet Carrier makes traveling easy and safe.

Although having your dog loose on the seat next to you may provide company of a sort on a long trip, it is extremely dangerous. Sudden stops or a rear-end collision can throw the dog against the windshield, resulting in severe injuries or death. Exuberant dogs think nothing of throwing themselves across your line of vision were they to see something of interest out of the window on your side of the car.

The safest way to travel with your dog is to have him confined to the rear seat of a passenger car or behind a barrier in a RV. Seat belts or a crate are in order. Don't worry about your dog not enjoying the passing scenery. Most dogs lie down in their crates and fall fast asleep without stirring until you make a stop. Nylabone® makes a Fold Away Pet Carrier that is ideal for traveling because it folds up for easy storage when not in use.

Identification and Medication

Most states throughout the country as well as Canada and Mexico will require up-to-date vaccinations against rabies. Crossing the border to Canada and Mexico will also require health certificates validated by your veterinarian. Be sure that your rabies inoculations are current and that your dog is wearing his rabies tag. That tag and some means of identification should be secured to your dog's collar the entire time you are traveling. Many accidents occur during road trips, and often the occupants of the vehicle are thrown clear of the car. A dog will be panic-stricken and the first thing in his mind will be flight.

Dogs have been known to run for miles from the scene of an accident, and owners have no idea where to begin the search for their missing dog. Either an ID tag, a tattoo, or microchipping are critical for the safe return of your dog. Tattooing and microchipping are the newest methods of identification. Tattoos of registered numbers are placed on the dog's ear flap or leg, and the registry can contact you if your dog is found. Microchips are very small computer chips that your vet can implant into your dog. The dog feels no

No Pick Ups

Once you hit country roads, you will proba-bly see ranch and farm dogs in the back of pick-up trucks. Nothing could be more dangerous! A sudden stop could send your dog catapulting through the air, and even if your dog is tied down, the sudden stop could easily break the dog's neck. Being crated in the back of a pickup isn't any safer. I've known of dogs transported in that method that arrived at their desti-nation dead from heatstroke. Always consider the health and safety of your dog first!

Keep your dog on leash at all times so he doesn't become lost.

discomfort at all, and the chip can be scanned and traced back to you. Don't think of leaving home before you take care of your dog's identification.

Your vet will also be able to advise you on any special precautions you might have to take that depend upon the area where you are traveling. Certain sections of the country offer the risk of tick-borne Lyme disease and heartworm. Some states have "dangerous dogs" laws that require the muzzling of certain breeds. Look into all these details before you leave home rather than having to do so while your dog cools his heels in the doggie slammer while you run frantically around attending to things that should have been taken care of.

Packing your Dog's Suitcase

Before you go to your first shows, you should practice getting your dog ready just as you would before taking him into the ring. Use every bathing potion, brush, comb, powder, and dryer you need to get him looking just right. Make a list of each of those items and tape that to the inside of your dog's suitcase or tack box.

Part 1

Make sure you have all the supplies you will need before hitting the road.

Toys can help keep your dog occupied during long trips.

A tack box is an especially constructed container that can hold all of the things you'll need to prepare your dog in the ring. Most exhibitors keep a full set of what they'll need in the tack box and replace the items as they are used. They can be purchased at your local pet shop or retail store.

Professional dog show handlers are on the road a good part of every week, and experience has taught them to carry everything their dogs might need both as a matter of daily routine and in the case of an emergency. In addition to all the cosmetic equipment that a show dog might require, there are a number of doggie items that should definitely be stowed in your dog's trunk.

• Food that your dog is accustomed to for the length of the trip, plus a bit more. Abrupt changes of food can cause severe diarrhea.

• Drinking water from home in gallon plastic containers. Water change can also cause digestive upsets.

• First aid kit.

• List of parks and/or rest stops along the way.

• Poop scooper and plastic grocery bags.

• Food and water dishes.

• Favorite toys, such as Nylabones® or a Rhino® stuffed with cheese or peanut butter, to keep him occupied in the down times or in the car.

• Current medications.

Rooms at the Inn

Not all hotels and motels accept dogs. Usually the premium list (described in the next chapter) issued by the club hosting the show you have entered will list the hotels and motels in the area that accept dogs. If you even *think* you'll be entering the show, make a reservation at one of those places that accept dogs at once. You can always cancel later if you decide not to go, but those establishments are the ones that fill up first.

The club giving the show has no idea where you might be coming from, so their only thought is to list accommodations within easy driving distance of the show site. Accommodations you might need along the way have to be arranged on your own. Driving until you are totally exhausted and then starting a search for dog-friendly accommodations may be an option, but it's certainly not a very attractive or safe one. Even

As part of your travel research, find a hotel that accepts dogs as guests.

Travel Savvy

The American Automobile Association (AAA) publishes catalogs listing accommodations throughout the nation, and most indicate whether or not they accept dogs. Travel agents are also able to secure reserved bookings and will be able to secure accommodations that will accept your dog.

Air travel with your dog is complicated and requires advanced planning.

Part 1

If you plan to enter a lot of shows, air travel may be inevitable.

though some establishments advertise the fact that they do accept dogs, this may mean only small dogs or that all dogs must be confined to their travel crates.

A city's local Chamber of Commerce can be very helpful in this respect as well. The Chamber of Commerce can usually provide a list of hotels and motels that accept dogs and may also be able to provide a list of local veterinarians. Vet's offices are usually aware of the local accommodations that accept dogs, and it certainly isn't a bad idea to have quick reference to a veterinarian anyway.

Traveling by Air

It's highly unlikely that you'll drive cross-country often, and if you plan to travel by air, the whole picture becomes a bit more complicated. Air travel is not impossible, but it is certainly not as easy as having your dog safely secured in the back of your RV.

If your dog is of the under-the-seat-in-front-of-you variety, your problems are less complex. Even so, you must reserve space for Bitsy when you make your reservation, because the airlines will only permit a certain number of dogs on board.

Your dog will have to be in an escape-proof crate. You will also have to pay a fee each way to put your dog under the seat in front of you.

Dogs that are larger than the under-the-seat variety must fly as excess baggage in the cargo hold of the plane. The cost involved varies by airline and seems to increase significantly with each passing year.

Air travel for dogs is no longer a unique situation with the airlines, because hundreds of dogs accompany their owners back and forth across the country each day. The Department of Agriculture estimates that approximately 600,000 animals travel by air every year. A good percentage of that number is made up of dogs and cats.

Part 1

The Air Transport Association reports that 99 percent of all animals shipped in the US reach their destination "without incident." Of course, that remaining one percent of reported "incidents" includes everything from minor complaints to the death of the animal, and the legalities involved represent a major headache to the airlines. Their lack of enthusiasm for transporting valuable show dogs is understandable, but makes it extremely difficult and costly to transport our animals.

At any rate, it is possible to have your dog travel on the same plane with you with more than reasonable expectations that the two of you will reach your destination safely. Dogs do travel in the cargo area of the plane. Although the cargo area is pressurized, there is no on-ground air-conditioning or heat controls. Because of this, federal regulations require that no animal be shipped by air if the ground temperature at either end of the flight is above 85 degrees or below 45 degrees.

Travel is not entirely risk-free for your dog. When you must do so, there are a good number of safety measures that will help increase the odds of a safe arrival for your dog.

Airline Travel Procedure

• Select the airline that offers the greatest safety assurances.

• Make an advance reservation. Most airlines will only accept a given number of dogs per flight. Reconfirm (and then reconfirm again) before flight time.

• Schedule a direct, non-stop flight. Connections, changing planes, and long stopovers increase the risk of loss and fatalities. "Red-eye" (overnight) and very early morning flights are least crowded and offer better temperatures.

• Many states require a health certificate signed by a veterinarian, and nearly all airlines will require one.

• The crate you ship your dog in must be an "Airline

Choose a crate that is approved by the airlines.

Proper identification for your dog is extremely important when traveling.

Approved Shipping Crate" sold at nearly all pet emporiums and can also be purchased directly from the airline. The Nylabone® Fold Away Pet Carrier is one crate that meets this requirement.

• Fill one of the shipping crate's water bowls and put it in your freezer the night before you ship your dog. Just before you leave home, take the frozen cup out of the freezer and place it in the crate. This will melt gradually and provide water for your dog for a longer period of time.

• Prepare the crate well. Federal law requires absorbent bedding on the bottom of the crate. You must also supply food and water in dishes that are attached to the inside of the crate's wire door. Tape a small bag of food to the top of the crate along with food and water. Include instructions for food and water effective for the next 24 hours in case of delays. You are not allowed to put a lock on the crate door; however, you can offer double security with bungee cords or tape.

• You must include a "Live Animal" sticker on the crate. Airlines have these stickers available at point of departure.

• Tape a sign to the crate that gives full information regarding contact persons at point of departure and destination with phone numbers and addresses.

• Have your dog wear a collar and ID tags. Regardless of how careful everyone might be, accidents do happen, and a dog can manage to escape from his crate. Include a telephone number on the tag at which someone can be reached 24 hours a day.

• Arrive at the airport early. Make it a practice to get to the airport a full two hours (or more) before flight time and go directly to the passenger check-in counter. Make sure the dog is fully checked in but insist that you stay where you can see the dog until it is time to transport the crate to the loading area.

• When you do arrive at your destination, your dog will be ecstatic to see you again after all those hours away from you. However, leave your dog in the crate until you get to a place that is less frantic and a bit safer than the airline terminal. Have a good sturdy leash with you in your carry-on bag and snap the leash on while your pal is still in the crate.

An Airline Shipping Tip

Airlines require the crate you ship your dog in to be large enough so that the dog can stand up and turn around. Don't construe this to mean you are buying your dog an apartment to live in. "Big enough" are the operative words here. A crate that provides just enough room protects your dog from being thrown side to side in turbulent weather.

Part Two
Show Business

"Right. Here's your acceptance speech.
Don't forget to thank the losers."

It's Show Time!

There are three kinds of championship shows—All-Breed, Specialty, and Group shows. However, the procedure for every dog show awarding championship points remains basically the same. The All-Breed show, as the name implies, holds classes for all breeds of dogs registered by the AKC. Specialty shows are those in which classes are offered to only one breed. The Group show is actually a show that offers classes to only dogs included in one particular Group—Sporting, Hound, Working, etc., as listed earlier in this book.

The All-Breed Dog Show

Your first All-Breed show may appear to be a total madhouse, with people and dogs running

There are three types of champion shows that you and your dog can enter.

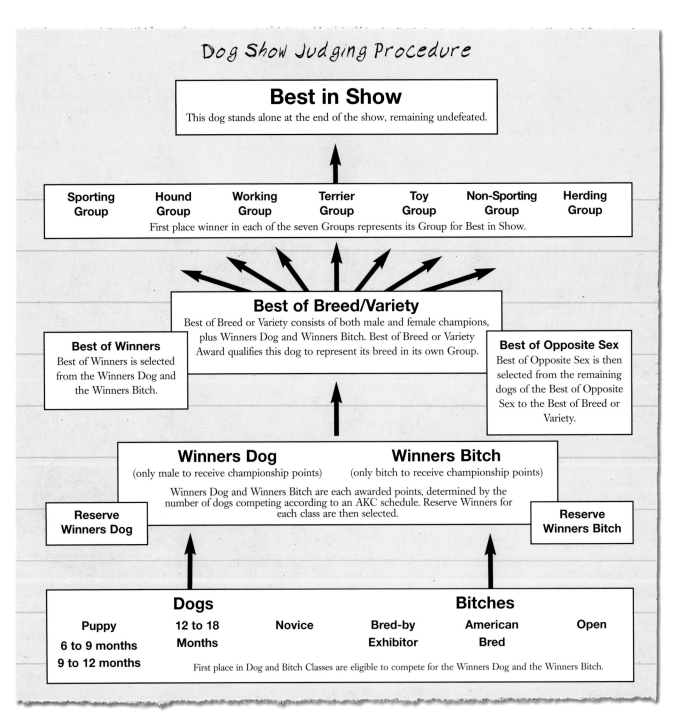

Dog Show Judging Procedure

Best in Show
This dog stands alone at the end of the show, remaining undefeated.

| Sporting Group | Hound Group | Working Group | Terrier Group | Toy Group | Non-Sporting Group | Herding Group |

First place winner in each of the seven Groups represents its Group for Best in Show.

Best of Breed/Variety
Best of Breed or Variety consists of both male and female champions, plus Winners Dog and Winners Bitch. Best of Breed or Variety Award qualifies this dog to represent its breed in its own Group.

Best of Winners
Best of Winners is selected from the Winners Dog and the Winners Bitch.

Best of Opposite Sex
Best of Opposite Sex is then selected from the remaining dogs of the Best of Opposite Sex to the Best of Breed or Variety.

Winners Dog
(only male to receive championship points)

Winners Bitch
(only bitch to receive championship points)

Winners Dog and Winners Bitch are each awarded points, determined by the number of dogs competing according to an AKC schedule. Reserve Winners for each class are then selected.

Reserve Winners Dog

Reserve Winners Bitch

Dogs   ## Bitches

| Puppy 6 to 9 months 9 to 12 months | 12 to 18 Months | Novice | Bred-by Exhibitor | American Bred | Open |

First place in Dog and Bitch Classes are eligible to compete for the Winners Dog and the Winners Bitch.

back, forth, and around. Until you get the hang of what's going on, proceed with caution–you may step on or get stepped on or crashed into by someone racing to get to their ring.

The whole affair is actually very well organized, even though it may not look that way. People there do know what's going on and where they should be. It just seems like everyone is running just a little behind where they should be at the moment. It's easiest to understand the procedure followed at an All-Breed dog show if you familiarize yourself with the Dog Show Judging Procedure flow chart.

Non-champions must be entered in one of the classes appropriate for their sex. Deciding which class to enter within your dog's sex depends upon the following factors.

• The dog's age

• Number of times the dog has previously won

• Maturity level

• Whether or not the person who is actually showing him on the day bred the dog.

• Whether the dog was bred in the US or in a foreign country.

Each of the classes you can enter along with restrictions that apply are described further along in this chapter.

Let's use a male Golden Retriever as our example. He is entered in the 6-9 Puppy Class. There are six other puppies in his class. The judge places the puppies in that class in descending order–first through fourth. Our Golden boy places first! The judge then proceeds on to judge the entries in all the other male classes. When the judging of each

The class that you enter will depend on a number of factors.

Best of Breed is selected from among the champions entered in the class.

The winner of Best in Breed goes on to compete in its Variety Group.

of these classes is completed, the first-place winner of each class will then be called back into the ring to compete for Winners Dog. This includes our Golden 6-9 Puppy Class winner.

The judge selects one of these competitors as Winners Dog (WD) and this is the only male who will receive championship points on that day. (It is our 6-9 Puppy!)

The AKC provides for any eventuality of error that might make the Winners Dog ineligible for his win. This is accomplished by having the judge also select a Reserve Winners Dog (RWD) to whom the points would be awarded if necessary.

This procedure is then followed in exactly the same manner for all the non-champion bitches entered. Once Winners Bitch (WB) and Reserve Winners Bitch (RWB) have been awarded in bitches, the males and females who have previously won their championships are called in for Best of Breed (BOB) or Best of Variety (BOV) competition. The Winners Dog (our puppy) and the Winners Bitch also return to the ring to compete in this class.

A Best of Breed or Best of Variety (see the glossary for the difference in these two terms) is selected from among either the champions competing or perhaps even from the day's Winners Dog or Winners bitch. Choosing one of the latter happens less often, but it is not out of the question.

If the dog chosen for Best of Breed/Best of Variety winner is a male, a Best Opposite Sex (BOS) will have to be chosen. As the name implies, this award will be for

Part 2

the sex differing from the dog or bitch that was chosen for BOB/BOV.

Finally, the judge must decide who is best between the Winners Dog and the Winners bitch for what is called Best of Winners (BOW). Once this is accomplished, The BOB/BOV winner prepares to go on to further competition.

The Best of Breed (BOB) winner from each breed then goes on to compete in its respective Variety Group. There are seven of these Variety Groups. They are judged independently, and the dogs showing are placed first through fourth by the respective judge.

When the judging of the seven Variety Groups has been completed, the first place dog in each of the Groups comes back into the ring to compete for Best in Show. The day's events are concluded when Best in Show is awarded.

The Specialty Show

The Specialty show is a show put on a by a club devoted to a single breed of dog. The show is conducted and championship points are awarded at Specialty shows in exactly the same manner that they awarded at an All-Breed show. The only difference is that there is no Variety Group or Best in Show competition. There are, however, many additional "non-regular" classes offered at Specialty shows. These classes offer breed enthusiasts additional opportunities to evaluate what lines within their breed are producing outstanding quality, and it also offers exhibitors additional classes to showcase their dogs.

Some breeds–Bulldogs, Golden Retrievers, Boxers, and Shetland Sheepdogs, to name just a few–have specialties at some place or another in the country practically every weekend of the year. Other breeds may have only one Specialty each year– the one conducted by the National Club devoted

A specialty show is sponsored by a club devoted to a single breed of dog.

Group shows are held for all the breeds in that Variety Group.

to that specific breed. The number of Specialty shows seems to rise in direct proportion to the popularity of a breed.

Group Shows

Group shows are actually a cluster of Specialty shows. In order to become recognized as a Group show, the organization must offer classes for every breed within that Variety Group. In other words, in order to be classed as a Terrier Group show, classes must be offered to every single one of the terrier breeds.

At Group Shows, the Best of Breed winner of each breed proceeds to the final competition in the evening. Although the final event is conducted like the final judging at an All-Breed show with placements for the top four dogs, the dog that places first would be considered as having won a Best in Show rather than a Group First.

Non-Regular Dog Show Classes

Show-giving clubs have the option of offering what are referred to as Non-Regular Classes. You are more apt to find these classes offered at Specialty and Group shows because there is usually more time available to conduct such classes. The requirements for eligibility are required to be stated in the Premium List sent out before the show.

Non-Regular Classes may be single-dog-entry (only one dog is judged as in a Veterans Class or Field Trial Class) or multiple-dog-entry (two or more dogs are judged together as a unit as in a Stud Dog, Brood Bitch, or Brace Class). The winners of single-dog entry classes, if

The Terrier Show

One of the oldest and most respected Group shows in the United States, if not the entire dog world, is the Montgomery County Kennel Club all-terrier show held in Ambler, Pennsylvania. The huge numbers (as many as 1,000 terriers) and excellence of the dogs shown there each year have made the Montgomery County show a role model for all other Groups to emulate.

Ch. Covy-Tucker Hill's Manhattan ("Hatter"), owned by Mrs. Jane Firestone
and Shirley Braunstein, and his handler Jimmy Moses winning Best in Show
at the Westminster Kennel Club.

The different classes allow dogs of all ages and levels of experience to compete.

otherwise undefeated in the show, compete for Best of Breed or Best of Variety. The winners of multiple-dog-entry classes do not.

Sweepstakes Classes

These are classes of competition offered in conjunction with regular classes, usually at Specialty shows for puppies or veterans. The show-giving club establishes class divisions, requirements, and conditions. No championship points are offered or awarded. The winners do not go on to compete for Best of Breed/Variety and invariably have an entirely different judge than the judge who passes upon the regular classes.

Veteran Dog and Veteran Bitch Class

The veteran dog and veteran bitch class is open to dogs and bitches seven years of age or older. This class is judged before Best of Breed or Best of Variety, and the winner is eligible to compete in Best of Breed/Best of Variety judging.

Stud Dog Class

This class is for stud dogs and two of their *get* (their puppies). The offspring do not have to be from the same litter, produced by the same dam, or owned by the owner of the stud dog. The class is judged on the merits of the get, not of the stud dog. This class is judged after Best of Breed or Variety competition.

Brood Bitch Class

This class is for brood bitches and two of their offspring. The offspring do not have to be from the same litter, sired by the same dog, or owned by the owner of the breed bitch. The class is judged on the merits of the produce, not of the

The Veteran Class is open to dogs that are seven years of age or older.

brood bitch. The class is judged after Best of Breed or Variety competition.

Brace Class

This is a class for two dogs of the same breed owned by the same owner. The dogs entered can be of either or both sexes. The judge renders a decision based upon how closely the dogs resemble one another with regard to soundness, conformation, size, overall type, and so forth. This class is also judged after Best of Breed or Variety completion.

Team Class

This is a class for four dogs of the same breed owned by the same owner. The dogs entered can be of either or both sexes. The judge renders a decision based upon how closely the dogs resemble each other with regard to soundness, conformation, size, overall type, and so forth. This class is also judged after Best of Breed or Variety completion.

The Brace Class is for two dogs of the same breed and the same owner.

Some All-Breed and Group shows offer Non-Regular Class competition. Those that do may also offer Variety Group and Best in Show competition for these classes. For instance, a Boxer selected best Veteran of a breed may compete further for Best Working Dog Veteran and Best Veteran in Show. When these classes are offered, they always appear in the show-giving club's premium list.

Premium Lists

All clubs sponsoring an American Kennel Club championship show must issue what is called a premium list. A premium list contains all the information you will need to enter that club's show. In most cases, a professional show superintendent sends out these premium lists several weeks in advance of the closing date for entries.

In order to be included in these mailings before you enter your first championship show, you have to advise the show superintendent serving your area that you want to receive all premium lists for shows that will be held in your area. Once you have entered your dog at a show put on by a particular superintendent, you will continue to receive premium lists for all shows staged by that organization as long as you continue to show your dog. A list of Annually Licensed Superintendents appears in the Resources section in this book.

The AKC Gazette

Until the time you have entered shows in different parts of the country, you should subscribe to the AKC's monthly publication, the *AKC Gazette*, which includes the Events Calendar supplement. This will keep you up-to-date on what lies ahead. Whereas premium lists are issued only a few weeks in advance of a show and are sent only to people on the super-intendent's list, the Events Calendar lists all shows to be held throughout the country many months in advance so that you can plan accordingly.

Receiving a premium list will keep you informed of the shows and their entry information.

The premium list will give you the date, location, and closing date for entries for a particular show. It will also list the entry fee, the judges for each of the breeds eligible to compete at the show, and the prizes that will be awarded in each breed.

Included in the premium list is the entry form that you will need to complete in order to enter the show (shown on the opposite page). Most of the information you need for the entry form appears on your dog's AKC registration certificate. The information that you enter on this form will appear in the catalog on the day of the show.

Required Premium List Information

Space is provided to enter the following information.

• Breed of your dog (and Variety if yours is one of the nine breeds so divided)

• Sex

OFFICIAL AMERICAN KENNEL CLUB ENTRY FORM

ALL BREED DOG SHOWS OF THE
APPLE VALLEY KENNEL CLUB
(Licensed by the American Kennel Club)
☐ **SATURDAY, MARCH 8, 2003** #2003222101
☐ **SUNDAY, MARCH 9, 2003** #2003222102
Mojave Narrows Regional Park, 1800 Yates Road, Victorville, California
MAIL ENTRIES WITH FEES TO: JACK BRADSHAW, Supt., P.O. Box 227303, Los Angeles, CA 90022
MAKE CHECKS payable to JACK BRADSHAW. FAX (323) 727-2949; website: www.jbradshaw.com; email: mail@jbradshaw.com.
ENTRIES must be received by the Superintendent not later than **NOON, Wed, February 19, 2003 PST.**
FIRST ENTRY of a dog at each show **$23.00** (includes 50¢ AKC recording fee).
Each additional entry of the same dog **$12.00**.   Junior Showmanship **No Charge**
Bred by, Miscellaneous and Puppy Class (6-9) and (9-12) **$15.00**.
ENTRY MUST BE SIGNED at the bottom by the owner or owner's duly authorized agent, otherwise entry cannot be accepted. I enclose $ _____ for entry fees.

BREED	VARIETY 1	SEX

DOG 2 3 SHOW CLASS	CLASS 3 DIVISION Weight, color, etc

ADDITIONAL CLASSES	OBEDIENCE TRIAL CLASS **NOT OFFERED**	JR. SHOWMANSHIP CLASS

NAME OF (See Back)
JUNIOR HANDLER (if any)   J.R's AKC NO.

FULL
NAME
OF DOG

☐ AKC REG NO.   Enter number here   DATE OF BIRTH
☐ AKC LITTER NO.
☐ I.L.P. NO.   PLACE OF ☐ U.S.A ☐ Canada ☐ Foreign
☐ FOREIGN REG. NO. & COUNTRY   BIRTH   Do not print the above in Catalog

BREEDER

SIRE

DAM

ACTUAL OWNER(S) _____
4   (Please Print)

OWNER'S ADDRESS _____

CITY _____ STATE _____ ZIP _____

NAME OF OWNER'S AGENT
(IF ANY) AT THE SHOW _____

I CERTIFY that I am the actual owner of the dog, or that I am the duly authorized agent of the actual owner whose name I have entered above. In consideration of the acceptance of this entry I (we) agree to abide by the rules and regulations of The American Kennel Club in effect at the time of this show or obedience trial, and by any additional rules and regulations appearing in the premium list for this show or obedience trial or both, and further agree to be bound by the "Agreement" printed on the reverse side of this entry form. I (we) certify and represent that the dog entered is not a hazard to persons or other dogs. This entry is submitted for acceptance on the foregoing representation and agreement.

SIGNATURE of owner or his agent
duly authorized to make this entry _____

TELEPHONE # _____

Part 2

• Class you wish to enter

• Additional classes if any

• Full name of your dog

• Registration number (check one box and include one of the following: AKC registration, AKC litter number, ILP number, Foreign registration number and country), date of birth, place of birth (USA, Canada or Foreign)

• Breeder

• Sire

• Dam

When entering a show, be sure to follow the directions precisely.

• Name(s) of actual owner(s)

• Name of owner's agent, if any, at the show

• Signature.

Read the premium list carefully. Double check to make sure the information you are entering is correct. Pay particular attention to the price of the class you are entering. Very often some classes, like those for puppies, are less than others. Entering the wrong information or enclosing the wrong among amount may result in your dog not getting entered.

Entry Closing Date

There is a closing date on the entry form of the premium list after which no entry will be taken. There is absolutely no leeway here. By rule of the AKC, a superintendent may not accept your entry after the closing date. Raging snowstorms, monsoon floods, and earthquakes will not mitigate closing dates. Send your entry in early enough and by a method that you will be certain of its timely arrival.

Dog Show Classes

These are the classes in which you can enter your dog at AKC shows. Each of the following classes is divided by sex, and all entries must be six months or older on the day of the show in order to be eligible for the class.

Puppy Class

The puppy class is for entries under 12 months of age on the day of show that are not champions. This class may be divided at some shows as follows:

Puppy Class 6-9: for puppies under 9 months of age on the day of the show;

Puppy Class 9-12: for puppies under 12 months of age on the day of the show.

Twelve- to Eighteen-Month Class

This class is for entries at least 12 months but under 18 months of age on the day of the show that are not champions.

Novice Class

This is for entries born in the US, Canada, Mexico, or Bermuda that have not, prior to the closing date of entries, earned three first place ribbons in the novice class or a first place ribbon in Bred-by-Exhibitor, American-Bred, or Open Class. Entries in this class may not have won any points toward their championships.

Bred-by-Exhibitor Class

This class is for entries being shown by any one of the breeders of record who is also an owner or co-owner of record. No champions of record are eligible for this class.

Pat Craige Trotter and her Vin-Melca dogs have won the Hound group a record 10 times.

Best of Breed competitions are only open to champion dogs.

If You have bred the dog You are showing, You can enter the Bred-by-Exhibitor class.

American-Bred Class

The American-Bred class is for any non-champion entry whelped in the United States as the result of a mating that took place in the United States.

Open Class

The Open Class is for any entry six months and older.

Best of Breed Competition

This class is for champions only, so you probably won't have to worry about this one for a while.

Reading through the requirements for the different classes, you'll undoubtedly see that they are organized with regard to an entry's age and prior accomplishments. The requirements don't say anything about your accomplishments, but take a word from the wise and consider these factors as well.

If you are a beginner, I strongly advise entering your dog in the appropriate puppy class if he is young enough. If your dog is over 12 months of age, enter him in the Twelve-to-Eighteen Month class. Dogs that will have passed the 18-month cutoff can be entered in the Novice Class.

If you've bred the dog you're showing, you can enter him in the Bred-by-Exhibitor class. As a judge, I'm always delighted to find that my winner has come from the Bred-by-Exhibitor class. Breeders are the mainstays of the dog game, and those who have bred a dog good enough to take the points deserve all the credit in the world.

The Open Class is for dogs ready, willing, and able to stand up against all competition with no excuses offered. It's where you'll most often find the strongest competition in both dogs and handlers. There's no need for you to start off in Open before you're ready, and a good judge will put up the best dog for the points, regardless of what class it is shown in. Then too, judges are far more forgiving of immaturity and lack of experience in the other classes I've mentioned than they are in classes that normally accommodate more mature dogs and experienced handlers.

Judging Schedules

Once all entries are in and accounted for, show superintendents are required to send a Judging Schedule to the owner or handler of every dog entered. Note that the superintendent is required to *send* Judging Schedules, but they have no control over whether or not the thing arrives in your mailbox. The mail being what it is, your schedule may or may not arrive before you have to leave for the show.

Be aware of the judging schedule so that you are in the right place at the right time.

The show you entered may a take a day or two to drive, and your judging time might be at 8:00 am. It would be a shame to have you arrive at your show to find judging of your breed had been completed. If you have not received your judging schedule at least a couple of days before you intend to leave for the show, call the superintendent's office or log on to the superintendent's website–nearly all superintendents have one now. The judging schedule for your show will normally be posted there five to six working days after entries close.

The judging schedule will give you the number of the ring in which you'll be judged and the time your breed is scheduled to be judged. Be at ringside well ahead of that time.

The schedule will provide the ring number and the time your breed will be shown.

Part 2

Let's say you are showing a female Akita. The Judging Schedule you receive will probably list the judging time of your breed in the following manner:

RING NO 5

JUDGE: MR. JOHN DOE

Ring Steward: Tom Brown

8 am

12 Bulldogs 4-4-(2-2)

9 Akitas 3-3-(1-2)

1 Bichon Frise 0-0-(1-0)

Most dog shows are separated into different rings for each breed.

The breakdown works as follows: The ring number in which you will be judged appears first, followed by the judge scheduled to judge your breed. The name of the ring steward assisting your judge follows that. Starting time is then listed.

The number before the breed name represents the total entry in that breed–Bulldogs in this case with 12. The numbers *after* the breed name indicate: total number of class (non-champion) males entered (in Bulldogs, 4), followed by number of class (non-champion) females entered (also 4). The first number in parenthesis indicates number of male champions entered (2) and female champions entered (2).

Akitas are scheduled to be judged immediately following Best of Breed in Bulldogs. There are 12 Bulldogs scheduled to be judged ahead of you, and most judges judge at the rate of about 25-30 dogs an hour. You could estimate that it would take a little less than a half-hour to judge the Bulldogs. However, you are required to be at ringside, ready to show, at 8:00 am.

There is no guarantee that all or any of the Bulldogs will be present. They could all be absent, and while you and your Akita fritter time away elsewhere, Rome could be burning–or at least your entry fee could be going up in smoke!

If Akitas had been listed as first breed to be judged at 8:00 am, judging of your breed would not be able to commence before that time. However, breeds listed as they are here indicate that the judge will proceed from one breed to the next without taking a break, and you are required to be present.

Identification Slip

Included with your Judging Schedule will be a slip that will serve as an admission ticket to the show and as an identification and confirmation of entry for your dog. There will be a number next to your dog's name. That number corresponds to the armband number that you will pick up at ringside from the ring steward before you enter the ring.

When You Arrive

Save yourself lots of frustration by copying the following list of "must dos" and look them over when you arrive at the show.

• Locate your ring. Set up your gear as near to that place as the rules of the club will allow.

Although the show may fall behind schedule, you are still required to arrive at the specified time.

Part 2

As soon as you get to a show, locate your ring and set up your equipment.

Make sure your dog is entered in the right class and that his information is correct.

Your armband should correspond to your dog's catalog number.

• Buy a show catalog. Look up your breed and check to see that your dog is entered in the correct class. If anything printed seems to be incorrect, find the show superintendent immediately and bring this to his or her attention.

• Check with the ring steward in your ring to find out when you can pick up an armband for your breed. You must wear your designated armband clearly visible on your left arm whenever you are in the ring.

• Make sure the number on the armband corresponds to the number next to your dog's name in the catalog. Any award the judge makes is noted by that number, and if there is any discrepancy, your dog may not receive credit for his win.

• Be at ringside ahead of time.

Problems and Solutions

So far, this chapter explains the kinds of shows you can enter and how to go about doing it. But let me give you a little advance notice. Everything that went like clockwork at home or at your handling classes will seem to fly out the window when you get to your first (or second, or even third) show.

Plan on tripping over your own shoelace in the ring, and you can rest assured that everything that your dog did in handling class with the utmost precision will be forgotten as he goes through the ring entrance. You're nervous, and that makes the dog nervous. You both forget everything you've practiced so carefully. Fear not–it happens to us all. The first time is always the worst. It does get much better, I assure you.

Poor Sports

Along the way you'll find most of your fellow exhibitors ready and willing to help you out when they can. There are, unfortunately, others who are rude and downright poor sports. They're the people who'll allow their dog to run up on yours from behind. They will attempt to pose their dog in a way that obstructs the judges' view of your dog. Their bag of tricks is limitless, and you will learn who these individuals are and how to avoid being near them in the ring.

It may be necessary to pick up your dog and ask the judge if you may go to the end of the line. If the judge asks you why you are moving, answer in as polite a tone as you can and honestly state that you are unable to present your dog to advantage because of what the exhibitor next to you has been doing.

Most judges will understand fully and will take great exception to such unsportsmanlike behavior. I think you'll find that when these ill-mannered people are called on their behavior in front of the judge a time or two, they'll stop trying their maneuvers.

Part 2

Ring Procedure

One thing that will help you considerably while you stand outside your ring is paying attention to the procedure that the judge follows. All experienced judges have a set procedure–where they want you to set up your dog to be examined and how they want you to move around the ring with your class and on individual gaiting.

I am always astounded to have an exhibitor who has been waiting outside my ring for what seems like hours finally enter the ring without a clue as to the procedure that I have been following. I have to tell him or her where to place the dog to be examined and what pattern to follow when moving their dog. The person must have seen me require dozens of dogs to do exactly the same thing over and over. I can only wonder

Every judge will have a different ring procedure that you should follow.

Win or lose—always remember to have fun and keep your perspective.

why he or she would think I would choose to require something different of their dog.

Most handling classes have their students practice the standard patterns of movement. (See the following pages.) The diagrams are included here so that you can practice them beforehand and will not be surprised at anything a judge may request. Do remember though, the pattern is the judge's choice and not yours.

Keeping Perspective

It's important that you maintain friendships and activities outside the dog game. People who have nothing else but dogs and dog shows in their lives become obsessed and lose perspective. Let's face it; if you don't win today's dog show, there's tomorrow and next week's show where it will all be different. It's not the end of the world. If you have nothing else in your life to be concerned about other than today's win, well, you'll be spending a lot of unhappy moments.

Regardless of who you are and how good your dog is, some days you'll win and some days you'll lose. It is just as simple as that. You have your good days and your bad. So does your dog. So does the judge, for that matter.

I know far too many people lose all sense of reality when it comes to their dogs and the dog shows they enter. They take every loss as a personal affront. You'd think the dogs were their children that they had to defend with their lives. They are able to see horses as horses and birds as birds, but when it comes to their dogs they see "little people," somehow an extension of their own egos. It's not a healthy attitude and I find, nine times out of ten, their dogs are as neurotic as the people who own them. Take all wins with joy and appreciation, never with bravado. Take your losses as a sportsman and congratulate the winner with sincerity.

Part 2

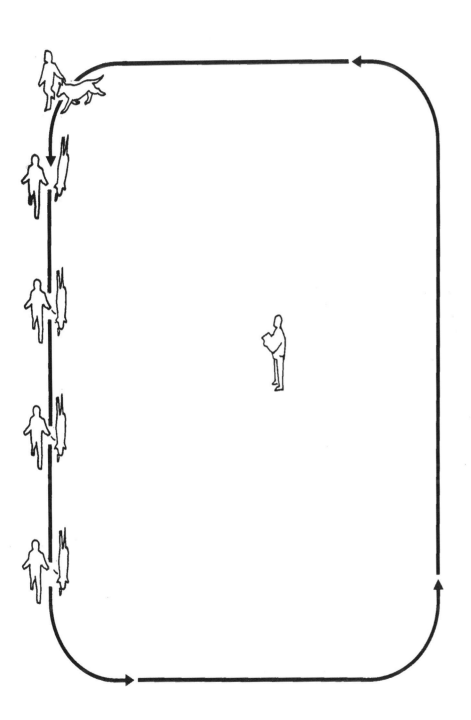

The Circle

After your class enters the ring, the judge will gait all the dogs counter-clockwise around the ring. As the dogs go around, the judge stands in one spot, usually in the center of the ring where he has a limited viewing area. In this pattern, the judge uses the viewing area to evaluate each dog, getting a first impression of general appearance, balance, and style as the dog moves around the ring. As you circle the ring, try to remember to keep adequate space between dogs and pace yourself so that when you move into the judge's area of vision, your dog covers that area without being restricted and moves at its best speed.

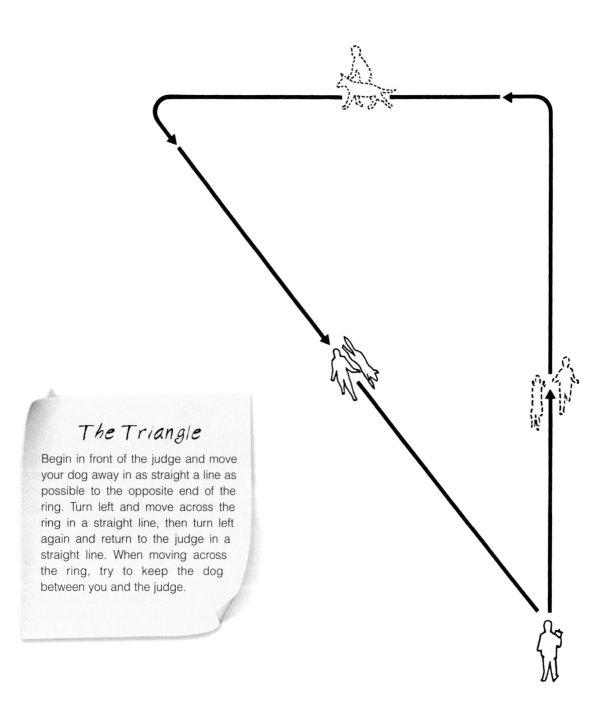

The Triangle

Begin in front of the judge and move your dog away in as straight a line as possible to the opposite end of the ring. Turn left and move across the ring in a straight line, then turn left again and return to the judge in a straight line. When moving across the ring, try to keep the dog between you and the judge.

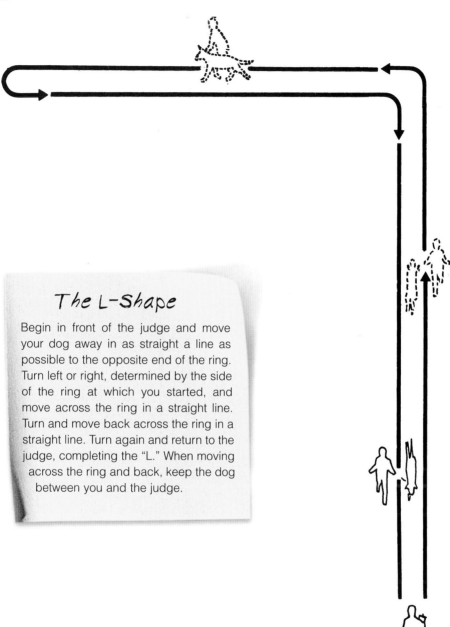

The L-Shape

Begin in front of the judge and move your dog away in as straight a line as possible to the opposite end of the ring. Turn left or right, determined by the side of the ring at which you started, and move across the ring in a straight line. Turn and move back across the ring in a straight line. Turn again and return to the judge, completing the "L." When moving across the ring and back, keep the dog between you and the judge.

Part 2

Straight Down and Back

This is the most popular of the movement patterns and the easiest to execute. Begin in front of the judge and move your dog away in as straight a line as possible to the opposite end of the ring. Without a break in movement, turn and move back toward the judge.

Words from the Wise

Lynda Gall
Lynann English Cockers

Lynda Gall of Newbury Park, California began showing dogs 26 years ago. She has maintained her modest but highly successful and influential hobby-breeding program through the years, while at the same time contributing to our country's future as an elementary school teacher.

Lynda began participating in purebred dog activities with English Setters and had great success. She has some 30 champions to her credit in that breed alone, most of which she showed to their championships herself. There have been 65 English Cocker champions bred at Lynann, and many produced by her dogs

Lynda Gall winning a Specialty Best in Show with one of her English Cockers.

have won throughout the country as well. Collectively Lynda's outstanding Sporting Dogs have won International Bests in Show, Specialty Bests in Show, and countless Groups and Group Placements throughout the US.

Lynda's advice to beginners is particularly significant because she has had outstanding accomplishments with her English Cockers, despite the fact that the breed is not one that is normally considered a powerhouse contender for Sporting Group awards. She has proven that knowledgeable judges will always give consideration to quality dogs presented to their best advantage.

When asked what she would consider the most important ingredients are in any beginner's recipe for success Lynda immediately responded with these three:

√ Finding a Mentor

√ Ring Presence

√ Conditioning and Grooming

She went on to say, "Each and every one of the aforementioned is important when you are first starting out, but having a mentor is without a doubt the first step to success and winning.

"It is important for you to do your homework in order to find someone who has been successful and is willing to mentor you. The mentor will have had their share of successes and disappointments in the ring. However, if you do not have the opportunity to have a mentor, then you must learn as much as you can from other successful exhibitors, owner handlers, and professional handlers.

"Go to shows just to observe these people. Many exhibitors and owner-handlers would be more than happy to help you learn. Introduce yourself and let them know that you are just getting started and would like to talk to them when they have the time.

"Talk to the professionals, but not during their busy workday. Ask them when a good time to talk might be for them, and if they would mind answering some questions you have on how to present your dog to its best advantage. A word of caution here–some professional handlers are very good about answering your questions, others don't have the time or just don't want to share. If you get a negative response–don't be discouraged; simply ask someone else."

Lynda also addresses how you and your dog appear in the ring: "Ring presence is another very important aspect of showing your own dog. Dress for success! Again watch the professionals–you won't see them dressing in jeans.

"Suits are the order of the day. For women a nice pantsuit is fine, but I like to wear a nice business suit. Finding them with pockets (for bait!) is the challenge. The colors of the clothes you wear are also important. Wearing a dark suit when showing a dark-colored dog or light clothes with a white or light-colored dog will detract from your dog. The judge should be able to focus on your dog easily no matter how far or close he or she is to you. I love to wear solid color light or bright clothes with my English Cockers and Setters–particularly with the roans and blacks.

"Aside from your clothes you must know what you're doing in the ring. For example, to a certain extent, you can make a dog have a better topline or more angulation by how you stack your dog. It's called presenting your dog to its best advantage. Handling classes are a great place for you and your dog to learn. Most All-Breed kennel clubs sponsor a class once a week.

"Many judges will also help you if they see you are a 'newbie.' However, in the ring they only have about two minutes per dog to access each entry. Don't take up their time then. At the end of their assignment, ask what you could have done better to present your dog. They will give constructive criticism if necessary.

"Conditioning your dog is one of the most important aspects of getting your dog ready to win. Good muscle tone is essential. Exercise your dog by jogging with him or her or by playing ball or going for walks. It really doesn't take too much effort to keep a dog in shape. (Oh, that we could say that about ourselves!) Make sure your dog is not to fat or to thin.

"Condition from the inside as well as the outside of your dog. Feed your dog a good balanced diet. Keeping the coat clean and vermin free. Even one flea can cause damage to a dog's coat, especially if the dog is allergic to them. Once the allergic reaction starts, it could be weeks before you stop the itching coat-damaging cycle."

Part 2

The Big Time

It's time again–time to pull out that objectivity yardstick and put it to work. You've used it for finding the right dog and accessing your own ability as a handler. You've learned to quickly figure out where your competition was good and where your dog was better. It may have taken a while, but you've also learned the tricks of the trade and were able to cover up those shortcomings you wish your dog didn't have while capitalizing on your dog's strengths.

Think back on your first shaky day at an All-Breed show. Quite different now, isn't it? Sure, the adrenaline still pumps when you're competing, but that's what helps you to keep aware and on your toes.

With wins and championship points under your belt, you're ready for the big time.

It's exciting to have your hard work pay off with a victory in the show ring.

By this time you may already have your first champion and those Best of Breed rosettes–perhaps even the Group and Best in Show–are looking mighty appealing. Competing in the big ring in the evening finals can be a thrilling experience, especially when you have done all the work to get your dog there.

Your question now has to be whether or not your new champion will fit the bill required to bring home the top awards you're after. Making this assessment is a difficult reality to come to terms with, particularly when you've done fairly well in the classes. What's important to understand is that just as not all dogs are worthy of championships, neither are all champions Group and Best in Show material. This is a reality that some exhibitors never seem able to grasp. The dog capable of bringing home those top awards is unique among purebred dogs. The Best in Show dog possesses a unique combination of qualities that is hard to find in the same dog.

I published a magazine called *Kennel Review* for a period of 30 years until my retirement in 1992. It was a monthly publication that catered to the top-winning dogs of all breeds throughout the country. This put me in constant contact with the kind of dog it took to earn the win records that many people like to compete for. I've also had the good fortune of being able to breed and own a number of dogs that compiled enviable show records.

Some of these dogs had more extensive records than others, but when it came to evaluating dog for dog within this group, without fail, the dogs who excelled were of breed type, a subject covered in earlier chapters.

The Dog of Great Type

I've made a lifelong study of just what this term means. I consider it so important that I wrote a whole book about the subject. In the process of coming to my own understanding of the term, I developed a definition of the word that best suits all the unusually fine dogs

Part 2

A great dog is the most important factor in the winning equation. Norma Hamilton makes it clear that showing an Irish Setter properly is a hands-on proposition. The manner in which she presents Ch. Quailmoor Jumpin' Jack Flash shows off his whipcord athleticism and alert nature.

Great dogs are natural showmen. Golden Retriever Ch. Gowrielea's Rant 'N Roar, owned and handled by Ronda & Rick Halfyard, wins Best in Show under the author as judge.

that I've seen around the world that could be included in that category.

A dog of great type is one that combines all five of what I call "the elements of breed type." Those five elements are: breed character, silhouette, head and expression, movement, and coat. The dogs I'm talking about here score well in each of these; the "greats" excel in all of them. They would represent what could be the epitome of their respective breed standards.

The degree to which your dog–any dog–excels in these five elements serves as a gauge by which you can estimate the probability of success. Your handling ability, some strategy, the wherewithal to support your endeavor, and a little bit of luck are factors to figure into the equation, of course. However, none of the latter changes the dog itself.

No doubt you've heard exhibitors say, "No dog has it all," or "All dogs have faults, even the great ones." There's truth in both these statements. No dog possesses every nuance of its standard. And yes, even the great dogs have faults, but as one of my mentors explained long ago, "The great dogs just carry them well."

Although there's truth in these old sayings, you can't use them to excuse the shortcomings that your dog might have. They aren't excuses for lack of quality; they are an explanation of how they can be carried by the best of dogs.

Great dogs are few and far between, but there are many who come close to that unique category, many with outstanding records but who are vulnerable when the going gets tough. Let's look at a couple of examples of what I'm talking about.

It takes enthusiasm and personality, in addition to beauty, to shine in the ring.

The Sometime Showman
Dog "A" is a Boxer bitch. She has a beautifully fashioned headpiece and the kind of proportions that produce the ideal silhouette. She stands square and

To a degree, a thrilling performance and winning attitude can make up for physical faults.

Some dogs really enjoy being in the spotlight.

compact and has the ideal proportions of her standard. She represents pretty much everything that you'd want to find in a Boxer of her sex.

However, her shoulder placement is a bit steeper than ideal, and she could use more hindquarter angulation. The combination of those two flaws doesn't produce the kind of free stride we'd like to see, and our Boxer girl isn't particularly wild about dog shows–evident in her lackadaisical attitude in the ring. Some days are better than others, but you don't know when they will occur. You can only hope they coincide with show day.

The Charismatic Dog

Our male Boxer, "B," is basically the right make and shape. Perhaps he is a trifle fine for a male, but he is at least near the ballpark. He could use a shade less length of muzzle, darker eye color, and a bit more length of leg. None of these are major flaws, but they are in important areas.

With these shortcomings, why would he have the potential to become a noteworthy competitor? Because he's an outstanding show dog. He has shortcomings in the type department, but no one told Boxer B this, or if they did, he wasn't listening. When he steps into the ring, his performance is absolutely electric. From out of nowhere, he puts an extra inch under each foot and hides the fact that he has a problem there at all. He arches that neck and is so busy challenging the competition, you never really notice he's staring them down with an eye that needs to be darker. He commands the ground he stands and moves on. He makes no mistakes in movement–at least none that are easily caught in the ring. To top it all off, his dark brindle coat is marked with a huge white collar and four white socks. Not required by the standard, but striking.

So, what's not to like about Boxer B? Judges who are first and foremost breeders at heart, and particularly those who know the Boxer breed well, would probably have difficulty carrying this fellow to the top, although they admittedly would have to give him plenty of consideration along the way.

Boxer B lacks breed type. His female counterpart lacks the things that put a show dog across when the chips are down–charisma, attitude, and eye-appeal. One judge–the breeder-oriented person–would probably go with "A", but when it came to Group awards or Bests in Show, he might well be forced to look to another breed for the final nod–a dog that was "really asking for it."

Another judge impressed by the male Boxer's presence would probably ultimately choose a dog whose type screams "quality" when pressed with a dog of another breed or even a better Boxer.

I'm using these opposite cases to illustrate my point, but I think it's clear what you actually need in what we call a Specials Dog, a dog that scores at least reasonably well in all characteristics that define breed type. The dog that has the highest scores all the way around is the dog most apt to be ready for prime time.

The $64,000 Question

In respect to your new champion, ask yourself whether or not he has enough of both type and charisma to make all the time and effort (to say nothing of the money) worth the investment. If your goal is simply to play at winning with your dog, and you are content to have your victories come when and where they may, you won't

A judge may choose a dog that seems truly excited to be competing.

have to be quite as critical as you would have to be if your aspirations were to extend beyond that.

Shooting for the Stars

You may be a real competitor and believe that anything worth doing is worth doing all the way. You have the dog that deserves to be at the top, and you have the handling ability. Now, all you have to figure out is how to get there. First, you might want to look at your destination point.

The Ratings Systems

Americans have an ongoing love affair with numbers and statistics. They want to know what the number-one car of the year is, what movie is number one at the box office, and which athletic team leads in wins, completed passes, and touchdowns made–ad infinitum. If you watch sporting events, you hear by how much a record has been broken right down to the millisecond. Not only that, you get the results practically while it's happening.

The Westminster Kennel Club holds one of the most prestigious dog shows in the US.

Dog show exhibitors are no less obsessed with standings. What dog ranks where on a national basis is as much the conversation at shows as anything else you might hear. There are standings that determine where a dog ranks in competition with its own breed (Top Winning Golden Retriever for 2003), within the dog's respective Variety Group (Top Winning Sporting Dog for 2003) and where the dog might stand in respect to all breeds (Top Dog All Breeds for 2002).

Wins are calculated on an accumulative basis for the current year. As each dog climbs nearer the top in its respective breed or Variety Group, owners publish this information in their magazine advertisements to let the world (and hopefully the next week's judge) know that this is one of the top winners in the country.

Commercial organizations, such as dog food companies and manufacturers of canine pharmaceutical products, offer prizes

Choose a goal for you and your dog and work toward it. Marilyn
Mayfield with her Best in Show winner, Ch. Grantilly
As Good As It Gets.

Every dog show in the US is governed by a ratings system.

The rating system awards points to dogs on the basis of how far they progress at a show.

each year for the number-one dogs at the various levels. The awards are presented to the owners of the dogs at awards dinners often held in New York City in February on the evenings preceding the Westminster Kennel Club's All-Breed dog show held in Madison Square Garden.

The Westminster Kennel Club show is considered by most to be America's "show of shows" and consequently attracts the important exhibitors and winning dogs from coast to coast. Thus the days and evenings surrounding the show provide the ideal time to hold the various awards dinners.

The original ratings system was devised by Mrs. Irene Castle Phillips Khatoonian Schlintz in the mid 1950s and introduced to the dog showing world in the all-breed dog publication of that era, *Popular Dogs*. Because she had devised it, her method of rating became known as "The Phillips System" and became the prototype upon which all subsequent systems have been based.

Referring again to the flow chart illustrating how dog shows are judged, you can see that the winners progress through a series of eliminations, starting with the first class of the day through Best in Show. The dogs first compete within their breed, the one Best of Breed winner competes in the Group, and the Group winner competes against the seven Group winners for the Best in Show award.

The rating systems award points (not to be confused with championship points) to dogs on the basis of how far they progress along at a given show. The results are obtained from the official records of the AKC. The count is based upon dogs in actual competition in the conformation classes, with absentees not included.

All-Breed Rating Systems

The All-Breed systems consider only Group placings (first through fourth) and Best in Show when it comes to awarding points, awarding one point for each dog over which the win is scored. In other words, if a Chihuahua were to win the Toy Group in which 100 Toy dogs competed, he would win 100 points. The dog that went second to him, say a Pekingese, would receive the Group total, less the number of Chihuahuas entered. Group Third, a Maltese, receives the Group total, less the number of Chihuahuas and Pekingese, and Group Fourth, a Toy Fox Terrier, receives the Group total, less the Chihuahua, Pekingese, and Maltese entries.

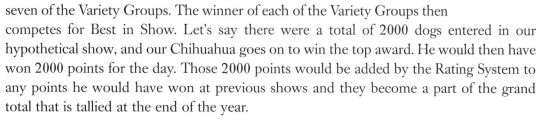
The rating points received are relative to the number of dogs competing in that group.

The points are awarded on the same basis to the dogs competing in and placing in all seven of the Variety Groups. The winner of each of the Variety Groups then competes for Best in Show. Let's say there were a total of 2000 dogs entered in our hypothetical show, and our Chihuahua goes on to win the top award. He would then have won 2000 points for the day. Those 2000 points would be added by the Rating System to any points he would have won at previous shows and they become a part of the grand total that is tallied at the end of the year.

If our Chihuahua acquired more points than any other Toy dog in the 12-month period, he would be considered the year's top Toy dog. If he were to win more points in the year's time than any other dog of any other breed, he would be considered the Top Winning Dog of All Breeds.

Breed Rating Systems

The same concept is used to calculate points for competition within the breeds. Because

The rating points are used to determine the year's top dogs.

the All-Breed systems only begin to calculate points for wins above Best of Breed, high breed standings can be more easily achievable, because the vigorous campaigns to win all the Groups and All-Breed Bests in Show are not necessary. Quite simply, a dog receives one point for each dog defeated by merit of winning Best of Breed.

Paths to the Top

Strategy comes into play here as well as it did when you began showing your dog. In a nutshell, you must be in the right place at the right time under the right judge.

With experience, you can begin to do a pretty good job of picking the right time and place. You may even know whether the judge presiding over your breed on a show day likes your dog. You figure you stand at least a better than average shot at winning Best of Breed. Perhaps you've shown to the Group judge previously as well and know you'll have some consideration there, too. If you win the breed, you stand a chance of winning the Group, or at least placing in it.

You know nothing about the Best in Show judge outside of the fact that she has awarded Best in Show to dogs of your breed in the past. If you get that far, you know your odds of winning Best in Show are no less than 7-1. Certainly, common sense would indicate that you enter that show.

The more clever you become at selecting the right shows to enter, the more apt you are to start compiling a record on your dog. Remember, however, that you are not the only clever and talented person with a good dog, particularly when you're competing at this level.

A really top-quality dog shown well in his own breed will stand a pretty good chance of winning, often right down the line. Showing your dog at this level brings you up against many outstanding dogs of their respective breeds.

George Alston was one of the most successful all-breed professional handlers for over 30 years. His wins include Group and Best in Show awards through out the US. Since his retirement, Alston has concentrated on teaching aspiring owner-handlers, and his students include some of the nation's top winners.

Improving the Odds

Is there anything you can do to help your dog shine in this heavy competition? I'll give you the same tips I used to give our magazine advertisers when they would come to me asking for suggestions. Advertising does help. The more winning that our clients did with their dogs, the more they had to advertise, and the more often the dogs advertised in our magazine were in the winners circle, the better image it created for the magazine.

If advertising is going to assist your dog's climb to the top, you have to have something to advertise, wins to present. You can throw your unknown dog into the thick of top-level competition and take your chances, or you can call upon that strategy we've talked about and get out of the mainstream to an area where the competition is not quite so fierce. This will increase the odds of your winning–perhaps something big like a Group or Best in Show. But even if your early wins are Bests of Breed or Group placements, you've got something to begin with. If those wins came under judges whose knowledge is held in high regard, it strengthens your dog's reputation.

An ad using a photo of you and your dog creates the image of the two of you as a team.

Use those win photos to start developing a reputation for your dog. Don't make exaggerated claims and predictions. Stick to facts and *never* make or infer disparaging remarks about your competition. There is nothing clever about challenging your competition to prove you are wrong or goading competitors into a battle of words.

In the beginning, make sure that you're in every photo that you use of your dog. You are trying to create recognition for the two of you as a team. Don't lose sight of the fact that yours is not the only dog of its breed out there winning, and with the amount of advertising that everyone does nowadays, who could possibly remember which dog is which? Your dog, on the other hand, is far more likely to be identifiable if associated with you.

As wins, reputation, and identification increase, you can begin using an occasional portrait shot or head study of your

Strategy is an important part of advancing with your dog in the show world. Sharon Newcomb has carefully selected the color of her outfit to compliment the red and the white of her Papillon, Ch. Copper Mist Ice Dancer.

Advertising is a good way to get your dog recognized by judges.

dog, but don't be premature in this respect. Thumbing through all the publications produced today, you'll see just how many winning dogs are being presented. The important advertising facts to establish are you and your dog as a team, winning accomplishments, and the caliber of judges making the awards.

Advertising and Judges

Does this approach to campaigning and promoting your dog assume lack of conviction or knowledge on the part of judges? In a word, no; not on the part of those who know your breed well. If your dog (recognized or not) doesn't meet the expectations of a knowledgeable judge, the dog will simply not win. No self-respecting judge is going to choose a dog who has been advertised over better competition simply because he or she read that the dog had won somewhere else.

A highly respected breeder-exhibitor I know told me something many years ago that is worth passing on. She said that advertising her dogs didn't make them any better as dogs or improve them in the minds of the judges who knew her breed well. Advertising the winning ways of her good dogs served to assure those judges that are not so familiar with the breed that what they suspected was a good dog, really was a good dog.

Words from the Wise

Pauline Schultz
Pawmark Bichon Frises

Someone once said that an outstanding Bichon is one part breeding and one part groomer's art. If this is so, Pauline Schultz has proven herself a master of both. Her Pawmark Bichon Frises breeding program has produced dogs of outstanding quality since the early days of the breed, and they have always been presented flawlessly.

Bichons became a popular dog to show among the professionals immediately upon recognition of the breed by the AKC. Their expertise raised the level of presentation to heights that only the very accomplished amateur could hope to achieve. Pauline Schultz evaluated the situation and learned quickly that she had two jobs as a breeder-exhibitor. The first was to breed dogs of such superior quality that they could stand on their own against all levels of competition, and the second was to learn to present her dogs in a manner that required no concessions.

Pauline Schultz with one of her winning Pawmark Bichon Frises.

Over the past 25 years, Pauline has accomplished that and more. She is truly a breeder-owner-handler of the master class.

Residing in Durham, North Carolina, Pauline has ventured forth to all parts of the country with her dogs and has claimed consistent victories against the best of her competition. To date, she has bred 68 champions, and has taken no less than 70 to their championships herself. The Pawmark dogs have accounted for 9 All-Breed Bests in Show, well over 50 Group Firsts, and 17 Class and Breed wins at Specialty shows.

When asked what advice she might give to a beginner who has a sincere desire to do well as an owner-handler, Pauline immediately replied that experienced mentors were invaluable. "Mentors—both in your breed and someone outside of it," she said. "The former to put you in touch with the nuances of breed type, and the latter to help you to understand the rules of canine construction and locomotion that apply to all breeds."

Pauline considers participating in the activities of one's own breed of great value. She also feels strongly that an owner-handler should be active in all-breed clubs and activities to maintain a sense of objectivity and keep abreast of important changes and developments throughout purebred dogs.

Other Shows and Events

The main purpose of this book is to prepare owners to show their dogs well at conformation dog shows, though the opportunities for dog and owner to do things together and to test their abilities are not limited. There are a vast array of other shows and events within the confines of the dog game.

Breed clubs often strongly encourage owners to help retain the versatility of their breeds by seeking titles in all aspects suitable to their respective breeds, not just in conformation. Dual champions, dogs who have won titles in both conformation shows and field trials, are highly prized among owners of sporting dogs. Many feel dogs capable of doing so represent the very essence of why the

There is a vast array of events in which you and your dog can compete.

Most events are designed to highlight a dog's natural abilities.

Obedience is judged on how well your dog performs a series of set exercises

breed was created in the first place.

Earning performance titles are not limited to the sporting dogs by any means. Many of these marks of versatility are available to dogs of almost any breed—all that's required is an ability to perform the standard tests. The following are just a few of the areas that owners can pursue in addition to conformation shows.

Obedience

Obedience trials are held at both championship shows and at matches. The same informal entry procedures that apply to conformation matches apply here as well. The championship, or "sanctioned," obedience trials are normally held in conjunction with conformation shows and also require pre-entry. They're handled in a much more formal manner than the matches are.

Obedience classes are definitely a prerequisite. Obedience competition is highly precise and based on how well your dog performs a set series of exercises. The exercises required in the different classes of competition range from the basics to the more complicated. Novice Class competition includes exercises like heel, sit, and lie down. The high-level Utility Dog and Utility Dog Excellent have far more sophisticated exercises requiring scent discrimination and directed jumping.

Each level has a degree that is earned after attaining qualifying scores at a given number of shows. The competition levels and corresponding degrees include: Novice, which earns a Companion Dog degree (CD); Open, which earns the Companion Dog Excellent degree (CDX); and Utility, which earns the Utility Dog and Utility

Dog Excellent degrees (UD and UDX).

The degree to which your dog responds to obedience training varies with breed and individual. Some breeds take to obedience with absolutely overwhelming enthusiasm, while others perform adequately, but it's a rare exception that any dog is incapable of achieving a Companion Dog or Companion Dog Excellent degree. Who knows, your dog could well be the breed's next obedience superstar.

Don't let the rules, regulations, and titles intimidate you. Actually, obedience competition follows in a very logical order that makes competing easy to learn and easy to follow. The training classes come first, and even if you decide you do not want to enter actual shows, what you and your dog learn in obedience training is priceless.

Basic training is a prerequisite for participating in obedience.

Canine Good Citizen® Test

This test was created for all dogs, not just purebreds, and contains the basics that you and your dog should learn if you're even thinking about showing in conformation shows. Nearly everything in the test is required of all dogs that attend a conformation dog show.

The purpose of this test is to demonstrate that your dog is well mannered and an asset to the community. There are ten parts to the test and a dog has to pass all ten in order to be awarded a certificate.

• Accepting a friendly stranger. The dog has to allow a

These dogs and their handlers show off in an obedience demonstration.

A canine good citizen will sit politely for grooming and petting.

Your dog should be able to walk calmly through a crowd.

friendly stranger to approach and speak to his owner.

• Sitting politely for petting. A friendly stranger must be able to approach and touch the dog.

• Appearance and grooming. The dog must be clean and well-groomed, and appear to be free of any parasites.

• Walking on a loose lead. The dog has to walk along attentively on leash without pulling.

• Walking through a crowd. The dog is required to walk along, paying attention to the handler without interfering with other people or dogs.

• Sitting and lying down on command and staying in place. The dog has to respond to each of the handler's commands.

• Coming when called. After being put into a sit or down position 10 feet away, the dog has to return to the handler when called.

• Having a positive reaction to another dog. The dog has to keep his attention focused on the handler in the presence of another dog.

• Having a calm reaction to distractions. The dog has to remain in control and focused on the handler in spite a loud or unusual noises, bicycles, or unusual objects.

• Supervised separation. The dog has to wait calmly on leash held by a stranger while his handler is out of sight.

If your dog successfully completes all of the required

exercises, he will be awarded the Canine Good Citizen® title, receive a certificate issued by the AKC, and have the designation CGC officially added after the dog's registered name.

Agility

Agility competition is basically an obstacle course for dogs, either purebreds or mixed breeds. All people involved (and everyone who watches) always appear to be having the time of their lives. The sport has become popular at dog shows and fairs throughout the world. There are tunnels, catwalks, seesaws, and numerous other obstacles that the dogs have to master off-leash while they are being timed. It's astounding how fast and how enthusiastically most of the dogs perform.

Agility began in England and caught the public's attention when it was first presented at the world-famous Crufts Dog Show in London in 1978. By 1986, it was already a major event in Great Britain, and had caught on so well here that the United States Dog Agility Association (USDAA) was organized.

The enthusiasm of the dogs and the supportive roar of the ringside as their favorite jumps over, under, around, and through the obstacles lends an electric feeling to the event. The dogs seem to love the roar of the crowds as much as any performer.

It's obvious that being successful in this event takes a lot of teamwork. The handler has to act as a navigator to assist the dog in where to head next. Although the dogs do all the maneuvering, the

Agility is an action-packed sport that is fun for both dog and owner.

Most dogs are as enthusiastic about competing in agility as the spectators are watching them.

Herding trials allow the herding breeds to use their inherent instincts.

Herding tests are judged on a dog's ability to move and control livestock.

handler has to direct the dog. In order to add to the degree of difficulty, the sequence of the individual obstacles is different at every event. Both the AKC and the USDAA can provide additional information, as well as names and addresses of the organizations sponsoring events. (See the Resource section in the back of this book.)

Herding Tests and Trials

Breeders of herding dogs encourage those who purchase puppies from them to participate in herding events. They believe the trials help preserve and perpetuate the breed's herding instincts.

Herding trials are sponsored by several organizations, including the AKC, the American Herding Breeds Association (AHBA), and the Australian Shepherd Club of America (ASCA). Requirements and titles differ slightly from one organization to the next, but generally produce the same results. You can obtain details directly from these organizations

The AKC's events are open to dogs over nine months of age that are registered with the organization as a herding breed. There are three levels of competition involved in the AKC's program: Herding Tested, Pretrial Tested, and Herding Trials.

Herding Test

This test is quite simple, as it is designed to reveal the dog's willingness to respond to his handler and his ability to control the movement of the livestock involved, including cattle, goats, sheep, or ducks.

In order to pass the test, the dog has to successfully accomplish the following:

• Execute a stay on command.

• Follow two commands to change the direction of the moving stock.

• Halt the livestock on command.

• Come on recall.

Ten minutes are allowed for the exercises. The dog has to successfully pass two of these tests under two different judges, but no score is given–the dog either passes or fails. After passing both tests, the participating dog is awarded the Herding Tested degree (HT). This becomes an official title and can be added to the dog's registered name.

Pretrial Test

Once earned, the HT degree makes the dog eligible for the Pretrial Test. In this event, the dog must complete the following:

• Work the livestock through obstacles.

• Stop the stock.

• Turn the stock.

• Reverse the direction of the stock.

• Pen the stock within ten minutes.

This is also a pass/fail event and has to be successfully completed under two different judges. When the dog is successful, he earns the official Pretrial Tested (PT) title.

If he does well, your herding dog can move on to higher levels of testing.

Herding organizations sponsor trials throughout the country.

Herding Trial

Dogs competing in herding trial events have three options: A, B, or C courses. The three courses are designed to show different areas of working ability.

Each of the courses has three levels of accomplishment: Herding Started (HS), Herding Intermediate (HI), and Herding Advanced (HA). Proficiency in the advanced level earns the dog a Herding Excellent (HX) title, which is the highest degree attainable.

All of these trials have to be completed with a score of at least 60 out of possible 100 points, which are divided into six categories of proficiency. A dog must earn at least half of the points allotted to each of the six categories in order to qualify.

The courses involve complex patterns, many of which require a participating dog to respond to hand signals from the handler rather than to verbal commands.

Details of these complex trials can be obtained from the AKC's Herding Department, and there are numerous books and periodicals on the subject. The AKC also sponsors herding

Eligible Herding Breeds

These breeds are eligible to participate in herding trials:

Australian Cattle Dog	Bouvier des Flandres	Pembroke Welsh Corgi
Australian Shepherd	Briard	Puli
Bearded Collie	Canaan Dog	Rottweiler
Belgian Malinois	Cardigan Welsh Corgi	Samoyed
Belgian Sheepdog	Collie (Rough and Smooth)	Shetland Sheepdog
Belgian Tervuren	German Shepherd Dog	
Border Collie	Old English Sheepdog	

trial clinics at various locations throughout the United States through the year.

Tracking

Tracking events earn the Tracking Dog (TD) and Tracking Dog Excellent (TDX) titles. The tracking tests are sponsored and titles are awarded by the AKC, the United Schutzhund Club of America (an affiliate of the World Union of German Shepherd Dogs), and the United Kennel Club (UKC). AKC tracking allows any purebred dog to compete, and the UKC allows mixed breeds as well. There is some difference in test rules, so you should contact the respective organization.

Hounds have been accompanying humans on hunts for centuries.

The AKC offers two levels of tracking tests and their corresponding titles—Tracking Dog (TD) and Tracking Dog Excellent (TDX). These tests are open to any qualified AKC-registered dog that is at least six months old.

To qualify for the TD test, the dog must first have a certification of tracking ability by an AKC tracking judge. This usually entails performing on a standard TD track for the judge under conditions similar to those found at a real test, although a waiver can be obtained under unusual circumstances. The TD title is prerequisite for the complex TDX test.

The TDX requires the dog to track articles over a specifically laid out track that crosses natural or man-made obstacles over all types of terrain and cover. The dog must wear a tracking harness with a 20- to 40-foot lead attached. Once started, the handler has to stay at least 20 feet behind the dog at all times. The dog has to either indicate found articles or retrieve them.

Field Trials

Local breed clubs sponsor AKC field trials, which are designed for hunting breeds. There are always many helpful and enthusiastic hands at these events, and even novices without a dog to run can quickly learn a great deal by helping out at these club trials.

Search and Rescue

Search and Rescue dogs (SAR) are trained to find missing humans in a variety of adverse locations and terrain. Unlike tracking, search and rescue often looks for any track, especially in wilderness or disaster conditions. The dogs are trained to find humans, rather than the track or items, and if the SAR handlers can obtain an item owned by the victim, they use it to show the dog the scent to follow.

There are different types of SAR dogs, including:

Wilderness search dogs

Avalanche search dogs

Disaster search dogs

Urban search dogs

The National Association for Search and Rescue (NASAR) certifies search and rescue dogs, but many dogs can be used as SARs through local organizations.

Certain dogs can be trained to perform water rescues.

All field trial stakes are designated either as Open (for dogs handled by professionals and amateurs) or Amateur (where entries may be handled only by amateurs). The AKC defines an amateur handler as someone who, during the period of two years before the trial, hasn't accepted compensation in any form for the training of a hunting dog or handling of a dog in a field trial. Neither can any household member of a professional handle in an amateur stake.

Field Trial Classes

Open Puppy: This class is for puppies at least 6 months old but less than 15 months old on the first day of the trial. This class is to determine if puppies show a desire to hunt and boldness in covering ground and in searching likely cover.

Open Derby: In this class, dogs must be at least 6 months old but less than 24 months old on the first day of the trial. Entries must show a keen desire to hunt, be bold and independent, and have a fast and attractive style of running. They must demonstrate intelligence in seeking objectives and the ability for find game.

Gun Dog and Limited Gun Dog (Open and Amateur): Here the only age requirement is that the dog be at least six months old on the first day of trial. It is limited to Open Derby winners or dogs that have placed in any Gun Dog stake. Moving up the ability ladder, a Gun Dog must give a finished performance and be under his handler's control at all times.

Field trials are designed for sporting dogs that love to retrieve.

All-Age and Limited All-Age (Open and Amateur): This is where the dogs really have to know their stuff. Brains, instinct, obedience, and talent all come into play. Stake requirement is that the dog be at least six months old on the first day of trial, but this stake is open only to Open Derby winners or dogs that have placed in any All-Age stake. Dogs possessing all the requirements of the preceding stakes but style, conservation of effort, and experience weigh heavily.

What appears here just skims the surface of the various stakes and requirements, but owners who are interested in full details of the requirements can obtain them directly from AKC in the booklet, Registration and Field Trial Rules and Standard Procedure for Pointing Breeds.

Eligible Field Trial Breeds

Field trials are limited to Beagles, Basset Hounds, and Dachshunds, pointing breeds, retrievers, and spaniels. Each type of field trial has its own set of rules and requirements as to the performance of the dogs.

Beagles: Beagle field trials are the oldest of the AKC field trials. There are three types of Beagle trials:

Brace: two or three dogs track rabbits and hares;

Field trials are broken up into several classes for different breeds.

Pointing breeds must locate birds, point, and then retrieve them after they are downed.

Small Pack Option (SPO): packs of seven Beagles track rabbits and hares;

Large Pack trials: all Beagles at the trial, in one pack, track rabbits and hares.

Basset Hounds and Dachshunds: These trials are held separately, but are run in the same format. Both Bassets and Dachshunds are run in a brace (pairs) to track small game.

Pointing Breeds: Pointing breed field trials are open to Brittanys, German Shorthaired Pointers, German Wirehaired Pointers, Gordon Setters, Irish Setters, English Setters, Pointers, Viszlas, Weimaraners, and Wirehaired Pointing Griffons. The pointing breeds are run in a brace (pairs) to point birds. After the birds are downed, they must retrieve them and bring them to their owners.

Retrievers: Retriever field trials are open to Chesapeake Bay Retrievers, Curly-Coated Retrievers, Flat Coated Retrievers, Golden Retrievers, Labrador Retrievers, and Irish Water Spaniels. The retrievers must remember the location of the downed birds, call marking, and bring them to their owners.

Spaniels: Spaniel field trials are open to American and English Cocker Spaniels, and English Springer Spaniels. Spaniels must hunt, flush, and retrieve game.

Flyball

Flyball is a fast, fun competitive sport that is gaining popularity. Any healthy dog that can run and jump can participate in flyball. Teams of four handlers and four dogs compete against each other and the clock. Each dog must jump over four hurdles to a flyball box, trigger the box to release the ball, catch it and then return over the same hurdles to the finish line, where the next dog finishes the relay. Teams that complete the relay in under 32 seconds earn points. Dogs on the team earn one point for runs under 32 seconds; if the team's aggregate time is under 28 seconds, each dog scores 5 points. If a team is under 24 seconds, each dog earns 25 points.

The North American Flyball Association (NAFA) sanctions Flyball trials and awards titles to the participants.

If your dog likes to play with balls, flyball may be the sport for you.

Rally-O

Rally-O is not traditional obedience; it's not traditional agility; it's something between the two, but it stands on its own merits. In Rally classes, which may be either timed or untimed, the team of dog and handler move continously and perform exercises indicated by a sign at each location. The exercises include halt, left turn, right turn, U-turn, spirals, figure eights, and jumping, as well as basic obedience commands.

After the Judge's forward command, the team is on its own to complete the entire sequence correctly. Handlers are permitted to talk to or praise their dogs, to clap their hands or pat their legs, or to use any other verbal means of encouragement. However, they are not permitted to touch their dogs or to make corrections with the leash. Each course can have no more than five breaks or stops in the flow of the course of action.

Basic obedience training is necessary if you want to compete in Rally-O.

Points are given for each fault in the sequence. Timed courses are judged by taking the run time and adding any fault points to the score. Non-timed courses are judged by subtracting any fault points from 200.

Any breed of dog over six months of age, including mixed breeds, can compete in Rally-O. The website of the Association of Pet Dog Trainers (www.apdt.com) has more information on how to get started.

Therapy Work

A pet's healing effects are well known to the many volunteers that participate in therapy work. Therapy dogs provide positive support for patients in hospitals, at nursing homes, and at other care facilities. Dogs can often help withdrawn patients become less reclusive and more cooperative. They often form very special bonds and friendships with the therapy dogs.

Therapy dogs bring joy into many people's lives.

Therapy dogs do not require any special training beyond good manners and general obedience. Temperament is very important, and if you would like to do therapy work, your dog should become used to having strange people pet and touch him. Organizations such as the Delta Society and Therapy Dogs International require that your dog pass a modified version of the Canine Good Citizen test. Delta Society Pet Partners also require that prospective therapy dogs owners complete the Pet Partners Team Training Course.

Whatever you decide to do with your dog, whether it is conformation, obedience, agility or therapy work, the most important thing is to have fun. The time you spend and the training you undertake will only serve to build the bond between dog and owner and create a close relationship.

Words from the Wise

Kathy Beliew
Imagine Chow Chows

Kathy Beliew and her husband George live in Redlands, California. Their kennel name is Imagine, and it's easy to see how appropriate that name really is. Someone must be able to see himself at the top before they can ever have any hope of getting there, and "on top" is exactly where this husband and wife team has been since they purchased their first Chow in 1971.

They have taken at least 60 champions to their titles and bred or owned 7 All-Breed Best in Show winners. Kathy is extremely proud of the fact that she has handled all but one of them to those top awards. Collectively, the Imagine Chows have accumulated 26 American All-Breed Bests in Show and several hundred Groups Firsts. This stellar list includes the Chow that holds the all time win record for an owner-handled dog in the breed.

Kathy Beliew celebrates the Christmas holidays with one of her top-winning Chow Chows.

Kathy has had a passion for purebred dogs since she was in grade school. In 1968, she purchased her first show quality dog, a Great Dane. She began with a bang and not only finished her first Dane, but several others as well. In 1971, Kathy fell in love with the Chow breed and purchased a beautiful black female from Chia Hsi kennels.

In 1978, after a good deal of study and experience, Kathy bred her first litter. The litter included her first Best in Show Chow. Today Kathy holds the all-time breed record for the most breeder-owner-handled Best in Show winners.

Kathy is highly active in all facets of purebred dogs. She is Non-Sporting Director and Secretary of the Lake Mathews Kennel Club and Secretary of both the Sand to Sea Non-Sporting Association of Southern California and the Regional Chow Club. Kathy and George also enjoy the Hound and Working breeds–they've finished four Greyhounds themselves, and Kathy recently co-bred two litters of Great Danes. She's also on the Board of Directors of the Kennel Club of Riverside and has recently been approved by the AKC to judge Chow Chows and Greyhounds.

Kathy says that she wished she had lived near a professional handler when she was a teenager. Her parents were not involved in dogs, and although she says that professional assistance would have helped her learn the tricks of the trade far more quickly and easily, obviously what she learned on her own really worked well.

When asked what she might have done differently as a beginner, Kathy said that she probably "wouldn't have used a professional at all." (Her first two dogs were professionally handled.) Along the way, she also "learned the hard way" that cutting corners and making compromises didn't work–that there was only one way to get things done properly–"the right way."

Kathy certainly learned her lessons well on her own because she's become one of the country's most successful and highly admired owner-handlers.

Glossary

Achondroplasia
A form of dwarfism that affects growth in certain breeds of dog. Usually affected are the leg bones, so that the breed has a normal-sized head and torso but the legs are severely foreshortened. Examples are the Basset Hound and the Dachshund.

Action
A synonym for gait, motion, and movement and used in many breed standards in describing proper movement for the respective breed.

Agility trials
An organized event in which dogs negotiate a prescribed obstacle course.

All-Breed show
An all-breed dog show is one in which classes of competition are offered for all breeds of dog recognized by the registry governing the club holding the show.

Amble
Dog's gait in which the front and rear legs on the same side move in unison as a pair and alternately with front and rear legs on the other side.

Angulation
The angles formed by the meeting of the dog's bones. Usually in respect to the bones of the forequarters and hindquarters.

Back
Anatomically the dog's back begins from a point just behind the withers and ends at the loins/croup junction; more commonly described as the area beginning at withers and ending at the set-on of tail.

Balanced
Phrase used to signify a dog is symmetrically and proportionally correct for its breed.

Bench show
Dog show in which dogs are placed on benches while not in the show ring so that they may be more easily viewed by the public.

Best in Show (BIS)
Designation for best dog at an All-Breed show.

Best in Specialty Show (BISS)
Designation for best dog at a show restricted to one breed only.

Best of Breed (BOB)
Designation for best dog of its breed at an All-Breed or Specialty show.

Best of Variety (BOV)
At an All-Breed show, the award that is given instead of Best of Breed (BOB) for those breeds divided by varieties. (At specialty shows, the Best of Variety winners are judged in Best of Breed competition.) There are 9 breeds that are divided into varieties: Cocker Spaniels, Beagles, Dachshunds, Bull Terriers, Manchester Terriers, Chihuahuas, English Toy Spaniels, Poodles, and Collies.

Best Opposite Sex (BOS)
Once Best of Breed (BOB) is awarded, the best individual of the opposite sex is chosen to receive this award.

Best of Winners (BOW)
Winners Dog (WD) and Winners Bitch (WB) compete to see which is the better of the two.

Bitch
A female dog.

Bobtail
A dog born without a tail or one whose tail has been docked very short.

Body language
A dog's method of communicating their reactions and emotions.

Breed character
The sum total of all those mental and physical characteristics that define what a breed should look like and how it should act.

Breeder
Under AKC rules, the breeder of a dog is the owner(s) or lessee(s) of the dam of the dog when the dog was born.

Broken coat
Very wiry and harsh double coat; outer coat consisting of harsh wiry hairs covering a protectively dense and soft undercoat.

Canine Good Citizen
Basic test of a dog's good manners and stability. Passing the test earns an official CGC designation, which can be added to the successful dog's name on the pedigree.

Canter
A slow form of gallop.

Castration
Surgical removal of the testicles of the male dog. Also known as neutering.

CERF
Canine Eye Registration Foundation, which tests and certifies eyes against genetic diseases.

Champion (CH/Ch.)
Winner of 15 American Kennel Club (AKC) championship points under three different judges; 2 of the wins must be "majors" (3 or more points).

Coat
In dog parlance, coat includes amount, color, texture and very often trim.

Companion Dog (CD)
Official initial Obedience degree that can be earned by competing in the Obedience Novice class.

Companion Dog Excellent (CDX)
Next level in the Companion Dog Obedience degree.

Condition
A dog's overall appearance of health.

Conformation
Form and structure of a dog as required by the respective breed standard of perfection.

Confirmation
Official notification by the AKC of championship status or awards received.

Crest
The arched upper portion of the neck.

Croup
The muscular area just above and around the set-on of the tail.

Cryptorchid
Male dog whose testicles are not visible.

Dentition
Arrangement of the teeth.

Dewclaw
The under-developed first metacarpal bone and phalanges located on the inner surface of the pastern region.

Dog
Any member of the species *Canis familiaris*, or it can mean only the male of the species. To further complicate matters, dog fanciers are inclined to use the term interchangeably.

Dominant gene
A gene that masks the presence or appearance of an unlike gene.

Double suspension gallop
A dog's gait in which there is a series of gigantic leaps, leaving the dog totally airborne for considerable periods of time. Typical working gait of the breeds known as Sighthounds.

Dysplasia
Abnormal skeletal development.

Expression
The resultant facial expression created by the formation of a breed's head characteristics.

Free whelper
A female dog (bitch) who has her puppies naturally. Because of their conformation, the females of some breeds frequently require Caesarean section.

FCI (Federacion Cynologique Internationale)
Controlling body of pedigreed dogs in most of the European and Latin American countries.

Gait
The manner in which a dog a dog moves; distinguished by rhythm and footfall. Basic gaits of the dog are walk, amble, pace, trot, canter, and gallop.

Gallop
A dog's fastest movement. A four-time gait in which the dog is fully suspended once during each motion sequence. The sequence is right front foot, left front foot, right rear foot, left rear foot. See also double suspension gallop.

Gene
The basic unit of heredity carrying individual characteristics.

Genetics
The science and study of heredity.

Genotype
The inherited characteristics a living thing is able to pass on to a succeeding generation. Genotype is not always apparent in what can be observed in physical appearance.

Group First through Fourth
Designation indicates a dog has earned a placement in Variety Group competition at an All-Breed show.

Group show
A dog show open on to dogs of one specific Variety Group. However, all breeds in that group must be offered classes in order to stage a Group Show.

Head
In a general sense, head refers to skull-muzzle configuration. In dogs, there are three basic types but many variations within the three:
   (1.) dolichocephalic (narrow skull and muzzle, usually of great length as in a Collie or Borzoi.)

   (2.) mesaticephalic (typified by medium skull and muzzle proportions as one might see in the Springer Spaniel or German Shepherd.)
   (3.) brachycephalic (broad skull and short muzzle length, as in a Pekingese or Bulldog.)

Herding trials
Trials designed to test a dog's ability to control livestock.

Hip dysplasia (HD)
Abnormal development of the hip affecting the dog in varying degrees of intensity.

Hybrid
The offspring of parents who have dissimilar genetic make-up.

International Championship (Int. Ch.)
An award given only by the FCI.

Lure coursing
Working trials for Sighthounds in which they chase a lure around a course.

Malocclusion
An abnormality in the manner in which the teeth come together.

Monorchid
A male dog that has only one apparent testicle.

Movement
The action taken by a dog's legs as he goes from one place to another. The respective breed standard dictates correct movement for a breed.

National Research Council (NRC)
The company that researches ingredients before they are permitted to be used in dog foods.

Neutering
Surgical removal of the testicles of the male dog. Also known as castration.

Occiput
Ridge formed by the occipital bone at the back of the skull.

Oestrus (estrus)
Stage of the reproductive cycle in which the female will stand willing for mating.

OFA (Orthopedic Foundation for Animals)
Organization that certifies X-rays of hips and elbows.

Overshot
When the front or incisor teeth of the upper jaw extend beyond the front or incisor teeth of the lower jaw.

Pace
A two-time gait with the two right feet on the ground and two left feet in the air, followed by two left feet on the ground with the two right feet in the air. Both right legs move forward simultaneously, followed by the two left legs moving forward simultaneously.

Pastern
The region between the dog's wrist (carpus) and the foot (digits) below.

Phenotype
The physical appearance of a living thing; genotype as influenced by environment.

Posting
A dog's manner of standing in which the front legs are angled backward from the vertical. Also referred to as "rearing back."

Premium list
An advance notice brochure sent to dog show exhibitors that contains entry details for an upcoming show.

Recessive gene
A genetic trait that is not expressed unless matched with a matching gene and is completely covered in the presence of a dominant gene.

Reverse scissors bite
The front teeth (incisors) of the lower jaw extending so slightly beyond the front teeth of the upper jaw that the back surface of the lower teeth touch the front surface of the upper teeth.

Sawhorse stance
A dog's manner of standing in which the front legs from elbow down and rear legs from hock down are not perpendicular to the ground.

Schutzhund
German dog sport that tests a dog's excellence in obedience, protection, and tracking.

Scrambled mouth
Arrangement of the teeth in a misaligned manner.

Sickle-hocked
A manner of standing in which the dog's rear leg from hock to ground is angled away from directly perpendicular to the ground.

Silhouette
An outline portrait in profile of a dog. The proportions called for in a breed standard, or in its origin and purpose, establish the correct silhouette for each breed.

Snow nose
The pink or light streak on a dog's normally black nose that occurs during winter months.

Sound
Overall good construction and health of a dog.

Spay
Surgically removing the ovaries of the female dog.

Specialty show
A show restricted to only one breed of dog.

Specials dog (or bitch)
A popular manner of referring to a dog or bitch deemed worthy of being shown regularly in Best of Breed or Best of Variety competition.

Stacking
The act of posing the dog for examination or for having its picture taken.

Standard
The word picture drawn of the ideal dog of a breed that guides both breeder and judge in their pursuit of excellence.

Stifle
The knee join in the hind leg.

Stop
The juncture at which there is a step-up from muzzle to skull.

Therapy dogs
Dogs so trained as to bring comfort and companionship to hospitalized and elderly people.

Topline
The dog's outline from the withers to the set on of tail.

Tracking
Trials that test a dog's ability to track humans or lost articles.

Trot

A two-time gait in diagonal sequence—that is, the right front foot and the left hind foot are on the ground at the same time, while the left front foot and right rear foot are in the air. This is followed by the sequence of left front foot and right rear foot on the ground with the right front and left rear feet in the air.

Type

The distinguishing characteristics of a breed as called for in the standard of the respective breed.

Undershot

When the front or incisor teeth of the lower jaw extend beyond the front or incisor teeth of the upper jaw.

Unsound

A dog that is physically incapable of performing in the manner for which the breed was created.

Utility Dog

Advanced obedience trial degree.

Walk

The slowest of all of a dog's gaits; a four time gait—each limb moving one after the other.

Well laid back

Shoulders that are well angulated.

Withers

The top of the first dorsal vertebra or highest part of the body just behind the neck. Often referred to as the top of the shoulders.

Wry mouth

A bite in which the jaws are asymmetrically aligned.

Resources

Organizations

American Herding Breeds Association (AHBA)
Lisa Allen, AHBA Membership Coordinator
Phone: (508) 761-4078
E-mail: lisa@ahba-herding.org
Website: www.ahba-herding.org

American Kennel Club (AKC)
5580 Centerview Drive
Raleigh, NC 27606-9767
Phone: (919) 233-9767
Fax: (919) 233-3627
E-mail: info@akc.org
Website: www.akc.org

Foreign Registries
E-mail: foreign@akc.org

Foundation Stock Services (FSS)
E-mail: fss@akc.org

Performance Events
Phone: (919) 854-0167
E-mail:
Coonhound Events—coonhounds@akc.org
Earthdog Events—earthdog@akc.org
Herding Events—herding@akc.org
Hunting Tests—huntingtest@akc.org
Lure Coursing Events—coursing@akc.org
Tracking Events—tracking@akc.org

American Rare Breed Association (ARBA)
9921 Frank Tippett Road
Cheltenham, MD 20623
Phone: (301) 868-5718
Fax: (301) 868-6409
E-mail: info@arba.org
Website: www.arba.org

Association of Pet Dog Trainers (APDT)
17000 Commerce Parkway, Suite C
M. Laurel, NJ 08054
Phone: (800) PET-DOGS
Fax: (856) 439-0525
E-mail: information@adpt.com
Website: www.apdt.com

Australian Shepherd Club of America (ASCA)

P.O. Box 3790

Bryan, TX 77805-3790

Phone: (979) 778-1082

Fax: (979) 778-1898

Website: www.asca.org

Delta Society

580 Naches Avenue SW, Suite 101

Renton, WA 98055-2297

Phone: (425) 226-7357

Fax: (425) 235-1076

E-mail: info@deltasociety.org

Website: www.deltasociety.org

National Association of Search and Rescue (NASAR)

4500 Southgate Place, Suite 100

Chantilly, VA 20151-1714

Phone: (703) 222-6277

Fax: (703) 222-6283

E-mail: info@nasar.org

Website: www.nasar.org

States Kennel Club (SKC)

1007 W. Pine Street

Hattiesburg, MS 39401

Phone: (601) 583-8345

E-mail: skc@netdoor.com

Therapy Dogs International

88 Bartley Road

Flanders, NJ 07836

Phone: (973) 252-9800

Fax: (973) 252-7171

E-mail: tdi@gti.net

Website: www.tdi-dog.org

United Kennel Club (UKC)

100 E. Kilgore Road

Kalamazoo, MI 49002-5584

Phone: (269) 343-9020

Fax: (269) 343-7037

E-mail: hounds@ukcdogs.com

Website: www.ukcdogs.com

Foreign Organizations

Australian National Kennel Council

PO Box 1005

St. Marys, NSW 1790

Australia

Phone: (011-61-2-9) 834-4040

Website: www.ankc.aust.com

Canadian Kennel Club

89 Skyway Avenue, Suite 100

Etobicoke, ON M9W 6R4

Canada

Phone: (800) 250-8040 or (416) 675-5511

Fax: (416) 675-6506

E-mail: information@ckc.ca

Website: www.ckc.ca

The Kennel Club

1 Clarges Street

Piccadilly, London WIJ 8AB

England

Phone: 0870-606-6750

Fax: 020-7518-1058

Website: www.the-kennel-club.org.uk

Federation Cynologique Internationale

13 Place Albert 1er

B6530 Thuin

Belgium

Phone: ++ 32.71.59.12.38

Fax: ++ 32.71.59.22.29

E-mail: info@fci.be

Website: www.fci.be

United Schutzhund Clubs of America

3810 Paule Avenue

St. Louis, MO 63125-1718

Phone: (314) 638-9686

Fax: (314) 638-0609

Website: www.germanshepherddog.com

Licensed Dog Show Superintendents

The following is a list of Licensed Superintendents who send out information regarding upcoming shows for which they are responsible. You may wish to contact the Superintendents and request to be placed on their mailing lists.

BaRay Event Services, Inc.

Contact: Sheila Raymond

Mailing address:

PO Box 3075

Sequim, WA 98382

Business address:

203 S. 4th Ave.

Sequim, WA 98382

Phone: (360) 683-1507

Fax: (360) 683-6654

E-mail: dogshows@dbamlg.com

Website: www.barayevents.com

Jack Bradshaw Dog Shows

Contact: Jack Bradshaw

Mailing Address:

P.O. Box 227303

Los Angeles, CA 90022-0178

Business address:

5434 E. Olympic Blvd.

Los Angeles, CA 90022

Phone: (323) 727-0136

Fax: (323) 727-2949

E-mail: mail@jbradshaw.com

Garvin Show Services, L.L.C.

Contact: Jane Garvin

14622 SE Old Barn Lane

Boring, OR 97009-9267

Phone: (503) 558-1221

Fax: (503) 558-9236

E-mail: jane@garvinshowservices.com

Website: www.garvinshowservices.com

Roy Jones Dog Shows, Inc.

Contact: Kenneth A. Sleeper

Mailing address:

P.O. Box 828

Auburn, IN 46706-0828

Business address:

1105 W. Auburn Dr.

Auburn, IN 46706

Phone: (260) 925-0525

Fax: (260) 925-1146

E-mail: rjds@royjonesdogshows.com

Website: http://royjonesdogshows.com

Nancy J. Mathews
11423 SE Alder St.
Portland, OR 97216
Phone: (503) 253-9367
Fax: (503) 255-6734

MB-F, Inc.
Mailing Address:
P.O. Box 22107
Greensboro, NC 27420-2107
Business address:
620 Industrial Ave.
Greensboro, NC 27406
Phone: (336) 379-9352
Fax: (336) 272-0864
California office: (510) 724-4716
Michigan office: (248) 588-5000
Oregon office: (503) 649-8549
E-mail: mbf@infodog.com
Website: www.infodog.com

McNulty Dog Shows, Inc.
Contact: Eileen McNulty
1745 Route 78
Java Center, New York 14082
Phone: (585) 457-3371
Fax: (585) 457-9533
E-mail: emcnulty@mcnultydogshows.com
Website: www.mcnultydogshows.com

Jack Onofrio Dog Shows, L.L.C.
Mailing address:
P.O. Box 25764
Oklahoma City, OK 73125-0764
Business address:
3401 NE 23rd St.
Oklahoma City, OK 73121
Phone: (405) 427-8181

Fax: (405) 427-5241
Oregon office:
PO Box 4660
Portland OR 97208-4660
Phone: (503) 239-1080
E-mail: mail@onofrio.com
Website: www.onofrio.com

Bob Peters Dog Shows, Ltd.
Contact: Bob Peters
Mailing Address:
P.O. Box 579
Wake Forest, NC 27588-0579
Business Address:
88 Wheaton Ave.
Youngsville, NC 27596
Phone: (919) 556-9516
Fax: (919) 554-0519
E-mail: pete@bpdsonline.com
Website: www.bpdsonline.com

Rau Dog Shows, Ltd.
Contact: Kathleen Berkheimer
Mailing Address:
P.O. Box 6898
Reading, PA 19610-0898
Business Address:
235 S. 2nd Ave.
West Reading, PA 19611
Phone: (610) 376-1880
Fax: (610) 376-4939
E-mail: raudog@epix.net
Website: www.raudogshows.com

Kevin Rogers Dog Shows
Contact: Kevin B. Rogers
Mailing Address:
P.O. Box 230

Hattiesburg, MS 39403-0230
Business Address:
1007 W. Pine St.
Hattiesburg, MS 39401
Phone: (601) 583-1110
Fax: (601) 582-9909
E-mail: krdogshows@rogersdogshows.com
Website: www.rogersdogshows.com

Nancy Wilson
Contact: Nancy Wilson
8307 E. Camelback Road
Scottsdale, AZ 85251-1715
Phone: (480) 949-5389
E-mail: nancronw@aol.com

North American Flyball Association, Inc. (NAFA)
1400 West Devon Avenue #512
Chicago, IL 60660
Phone: (800) 318-6312
Fax: (800) 318-6312
Website: www.flyball.org

US Dog Agility Association, Inc. (USDAA)
PO Box 850955
Richardson, TX 75085-0955
Phone: (972) 487-2200
Fax: (972) 272-4404
Website: www.usdaa.com

Identification Organizations

American Kennel Club Home Again Microchip Program
Phone: (800) 566-3596

Int. American Veterinary Identification Systems, Inc.
3179 Hammer Avenue
Norco, CA 92860
Phone (US): (800) 336-AVID
Phone (International): (909) 371-7505

Sports and Games

Alpo Canine Frisbee Championships
Phone: (888) 444-ALPO
Website: www.alpo.com

Publications

AKC Gazette
260 Madison Avenue
New York, NY 10016
Phone: (800) 533-7323
E-mail: gazette@akc.org
Website: http://www.akc.org/pubs/index.cfm

AKC Family Dog
260 Madison Avenue
New York, NY 10016
Phone: (800) 490-5675
E-mail: familydog@akc.org
Website: http://www.akc.org/pubs/index.cfm

Bloodlines
100 E Kilgore Road
Kalamazoo, MI 49002

Dog Fancy
Fancy Publications, Inc.
Subscription Department
P.O. Box 53264
Boulder, CO 80322-3264
Phone: (800) 365-4421
Website: www.dogfancy.com/dogfancy

Dogs in Canada
Canadian Kennel Club
89 Skyway Avenue #200
Etobicoke, Ontario
Canada M9W 6R4
Phone: (800) 250-8040 or (416) 675-5511
Fax: (416) 675-6506
E-mail: information@ckc.ca

Purebred Dogs in Review
3 Burroughs
Irvine, CA 92618
Phone: (949) 855-8822
Fax: (949) 855-1850
E-mail: info@dogsinreview.com
Website: www.dogsinreview.com

Travel Publications

The Automobile Association of America (AAA)
Phone: (800) 222-4357
Website: www.aaa.com
Publishes US Accommodations catalogs, listing accommodations throughout the US. Most places indicate if they accept dogs.

Vacationing with Your Pet
Pet-Friendly Publications
P.O. Box 8459
Scottsdale, AZ 85252
Phone: (800) 496-2665
Website: www.travelpet.com

Internet Resources

American Veterinary Medical Association
www.avma.org

Air Safe.com—Pet Travel Resources
www.airsafe.com/issues/pets.htm

Video

AKC and the Sport of Dogs, American Kennel Club
Dog Steps, Rachel Page Elliot, American Kennel Club
Puppy Puzzle, Pat Hastings, Dogfolk Enterprises
Right Dog for You, American Kennel Club
Breed Standard Videos, American Kennel Club

Emergency Services

National Animal Poison Control Center
1-888-426-4435
Website: www.napcc.aspca.org

Animal Poison Hotline
(888) 232-8870

Index

A

Advertising, 184, 186

Affenpinscher, 44, 98

Afghan Hound, 40

Aggression, 106-109

Agility, 193

Air travel, 136-139

Airedale Terrier, 42, 98

AKC Gazette, 152

Akita, 41, 84

Alaskan Malamute, 41

All-breed dog show, 143–147

All-breed matches, 22

All-breed rating system, 181

Altana's Mystique, Ch., 78, 79

Amateur handlers, 28, 29

American Automobile Association (AAA), 135

American Eskimo Dog, 45

American Foxhound, 40

American Herding Breeds Association (AHBA), 194

American Kennel Club, 18, 20, 23, 31, 32, 36, 104, 151

American Rare Breed Association (ARBA), 19

American Staffordshire Terrier, 42

American Water Spaniel, 38

American-bred class, 144, 156

Anatolian Shepherd Dog, 41, 105

Anatomy, 82-87

Andrews, BJ, 84

Association of Pet Dog Trainers (APDT), 202

Australian Cattle Dog, 46, 196

Australian Shepherd Club of America (ASCA), 194

Australian Shepherd, 46, 196

Australian Terrier, 42, 98

B

Back, 86

Backline, 62

Baiting, 121

Banbury Benson of Bedrock, ROM, Ch., 33, 34

Basenji, 40

Basset Hound, 40

Beagle, 40

Bearded Collie, 46, 98, 196

Beau Monde Miss Chaminade, Ch., 85

Beau Monde More Paint, Ch., 122

Beauceron, 47

Bedlington Terrier, 42, 98

Belgian Malinois, 46, 196

Belgian Sheepdog, 46, 196

Belgian Tervuren, 46, 196

Beliew, Kathy, 203, 204

Bermarg's Sony of Boondox L, Ch., 123

Bernese Mountain Dog, 41

Best in Show, 144

Best of Breed, 144, 156

Bichon Frise, 45, 98

Bitch, 67, 68

Biting, 104

Black and Tan Coonhound, 40

Black Russian Terrier, 47

Bloodhound, 40

Body, 62

Bone disorders, 92

Bonnie Scamp of Wolfpit, Ch., 100

Bonnie Vamp of Wolfpit, Ch., 100

Bonnie Vixen of Wolfpit, Ch., 100

Border Collie, 46, 196

Border Terrier, 42, 98

Borzoi, 40

Boston Terrier, 45

Bouvier des Flandres, 46, 196

Boxer, 41

Brace class, 151

Braunstein, Shirley, 149

Bred-by-exhibitor class, 144, 155

Breed rating system, 181, 182

Breed selection, 47, 48

Breed standard, 17, 55

Breeder-exhibitors, 28, 29

Breeders, 24-26, 49

Breeding, 66-70

Breeds, 47

Briard, 46, 86, 98, 196

Brittany, 38

Brood bitch classes, 150

Brussels Griffon, 44, 98

Bull Terrier, 42

Bulldog, 45

Bullmastiff, 41

Buttocks, 87

C

Cairn Terrier, 42, 98, 100, 101

Cairnwood's Quince, Ch., 101

Campaigns, 68

Canaan Dog, 46, 196

Canine Good Citizen Test, 18, 191, 192

Car travel, 129-134

Cardigan Welsh Corgi, 46, 196

Cataracts, 92

Cavalier King Charles Spaniel, 44

Championship shows, 23

Chesapeake Bay Retriever, 38, 86

Chest, 62

Chihuahua, 44

Chinese Crested, 44

Chinese Shar-Pei, 45

Chow Chow, 45, 98

Clumber Spaniel, 38

Coat condition, 76

Coat, 64

Cocker Spaniel, 38, 98, 99, 122

Collie, 46, 98, 196

Color, 64

Conformation show, 20

Co-ownership, 72, 73

Copper Mist Ice Dancer, Ch., 185

Corrish, Geoff, 51

Cotman, Esther, 100

Courtenay Fleetfoot of Pennyworth, Ch., 52, 53

Covy-Tucker Hill's Manhattan, Ch., 149

Crate training, 111-113

Crates, 111-113, 137, 138

Crest, 83

Croup, 87

Crufts, 51

Curly-Coated Retriever, 38

D

Dachshund, 40, 123

Dalmatian, 45

Dandie Dinmont Terrier, 42, 98

Delta Society, 203

Dewclaws, 63, 86, 87

Diet, 95, 96

Doberman Pinscher, 41

Dog food, 93–95

Dog show superintendent, 29

E

Ears, 61, 83

Ectropion, 92

Elbow dysplasia, 92

English Cocker Spaniel, 38, 98

English Foxhound, 40

English Setter, 38, 52, 53, 98

English Springer Spaniel, 38, 98

English Toy Spaniel, 44

Entropion, 92

Entry form, 152-154

Etiquette, 110

Events Calendar, 152

Exercise, 81, 82

    adults, 82

    puppy, 81

Eye disorders, 92

Eyes, 61, 83

F

Feet, 63

Field Spaniel, 38

Field trials, 198-201

Finnish Spitz, 45

Firestone, Jane, 149

Flat Coated Retriever, 38

Flyball, 201

Food dyes, 96

Forearm, 86

Foreface, 60, 61

Forelegs, 86

Forequarters, 63

Free stacking, 121

French Bulldog, 45

G

Gait, 64, 65

Gall, Lynda, 167-169

General appearance, 58, 59

German Pinscher, 41

German Shepherd Dog, 37, 46, 78, 79, 196

German Shorthaired Pointer, 38

German Wirehaired Pointer, 38

Giant Schnauzer, 41

Glen of Imaal Terrier, 47

Goetz, Leon, 126, 127

Golden Retriever, 38, 58, 98

Gordon Setter, 38

Gowrieled's Rant 'N Roar Ch., 174

Grantilly As Good As It Gets, Ch., 179

Great Britain, 16

Great Dane, 41

Great Pyrenees, 41, 86

Greater Swiss Mountain Dog, 41

Greyhound, 40

Grooming table, 116, 120

Grooming, 96-99

Group show, 148

H

Halfyard Ronda and Rick, 174

Hamilton, Norma, 173

Handling classes, 124, 125

Harrier, 40

Havanese, 44

Head, 60, 61

Health, 88-93

    inherited diseases, 91–93

Henery, William, 52

Herding Group, 37, 46

Herding tests, 194–197

Hindquarters, 63

Hip dysplasia, 92

Hips, 87

Hock joint, 87

Hollycourt Miniature Poodles, 101

Hollyfir's Poacher's Pocket of Piketburg, Ch., 52

Holt, William, 53

Horner, Tom, 58

Hotels, 135

Hound Group, 36, 38, 40

Hutchinson, Lydia Coleman, 100, 101

Hutchinson, Susan Taylor, 100

I

Ibizan Hound, 40

Identification slip, 159

Identification, 132

Invitational shows, 23, 24

Irish Setter, 38, 98

Irish Terrier, 42, 98

Irish Water Spaniel, 38, 98

Irish Wolfhound, 40

Italian Greyhound, 44

J

Jack Russell Terrier, 42

Japanese Chin, 44

Johnson, Don, 122

Jones, Dan and Julie, 39

Judges, 26

Judging procedure, 144

Judging schedules, 157–159

K

Keeshond, 45, 98

Kelchner, Ruelle, 101

Kennel Club, The, 17, 19, 20

Kennel Review, 33, 172

Kerry Blue Terrier, 42, 98

Komondor, 41

Kuvasz, 41

L

Labrador Retriever, 38

Lakeland Terrier, 42, 98

Lawrence, Marion and Samuel, 43

Leasing, 73, 74

Legs, 63

Lhasa Apso, 45, 51

Lil' Creek Briarcrest Top Gun, Ch., 39

Loin, 62, 86

Lowchen, 45, 98

Lynann English Cockers, 167

M

Mackay-Smith, Wingate, 33, 34

Males, 68, 69

Maltese, 44, 98

Manchester Terrier, 42

Mastiff, 41

Match shows, 21

Mats, 121

Mayfield, Marilyn, 179

Medication, 132

Melbourne Royal, 51

Mentors, 71

Microchipping, 132

Miniature Bull Terrier, 42

Miniature Pinscher, 44

Miniature Schnauzer, 42, 98

Miscellaneous Class, 46, 47

Montgomery County Kennel Club, 148

Moses, Jimmy, 78, 79, 149

Motels, 135

Motion sickness, 113

Movement, 65

Muzzle, 60, 61, 83

N

National Association for Search and Rescue (NASAR), 198

Neapolitan Mastiff, 47

Neck, 62, 83

Neutering, 92

Newcastle-upon-Tyne, 16, 17

Newcomb, Sharon, 105, 185

Newcombe, Margaret, 53

Newfoundland, 41

Non-regular dog show classes, 148–151

Non-Sporting Group, 37, 45

Norfolk Terrier, 42, 98

North American Flyball Association (NAFA), 201

Norwegian Elkhound, 40

Norwich Terrier, 42, 98

Nose, 61, 83

Nova Scotia Duck Tolling Retriever, 38

Novice class, 144, 155

Nutrition, 93

O

Obedience, 190, 191

Occiput, 83

Old English Sheepdog, 46, 98, 196

Oosthuizen, Peet, 52

Open class, 144, 156

Osteosarcoma, 92

Otterhound, 40

P

Pads, 87

Papillon, 44

Pasterns, 63

Patella luxation, 92

Pawmark Bichon Frises, 187, 188

Pekingese, 44, 98

Pelvis, 86

Pembroke Welsh Corgi, 46, 196

Petit Basset Griffon Vendeen, 40

Pharaoh Hound, 40

Phillips System, The, 180

Plotthound, 47

Pointer, 38

Pomeranian, 44, 98

Poodle, 45, 98

Popular Dogs, 180

Portuguese Water Dog, 41

Powers, Barbara, 123

Premium list, 151

Professional handlers, 28

Proportion, 59, 60

Pug, 44

Puli, 46, 98, 196

Puppy class, 144, 155

Q

Quailmoor Jumpin' Jack Flash, Ch., 173

R

Rally-O, 201, 202

Rating system, 178, 181, 182

Rear pasterns, 87

Redbone Coonhound, 47

Registry's Lonesome Dove, Ch., 43

Reverie Australian Shepherds, 126

Rhodesian Ridgeback, 40

Ribs, 62

Ring patterns, 162-166

    straight down and back, 166

    the circle, 163

    the L shape, 165

    the triangle, 164

Ring procedure, 161-166

Ring stewards, 27

Rock Falls Colonel, Ch., 52, 53

Rottweiler, 41, 196

S

Saint Bernard, 41

Saluki, 40

Samoyed, 41, 196

Saxonspring's Fresno, Ch., 51

Schipperke, 45

Schlintz, Irene Castle Phillips Khatoonian, 180

Schultz, Pauline, 187

Scottish Deerhound, 40

Scottish Terrier, 42, 98

Sealyham Terrier, 42, 98

Search and Rescue dogs, 198

Shetland Sheepdog, 46, 98, 196

Shiba Inu, 45

Shih Tzu, 44, 98

Shoulders, 83

Show dogs, 66, 70, 71

    breeding, 66-70

    buying, 70, 71

Siberian Husky, 41

Silky Terrier, 44

Silverwood's Texas Justice, Ch., 126

Size, 59, 60

Skull, 83

Skye Terrier, 42, 98

Smooth Fox Terrier, 42

Socialization, 106, 109

Soft Coated Wheaten Terrier, 42, 98

Soundness, 76, 86

Spaying, 92

Specialty matches, 22

Specialty show, 147148

Spinone Italiano, 38

Sporting Group, 36, 38

Stacking, 117-120

    free, 121

Standard Schnauzer, 41

States Kennel Club, 19

Stifle joint, 87

Stop, 60, 61, 83

Stubbs, Barbara B., 85

Stud dog classes, 150

Substance, 59, 60

Sweepstake classes, 150

T

Table manners, 115, 117

Table, judging, 115, 117

Tail, 62, 63, 86

Tanner, Troy, 52

Tattooing, 132

Team class, 151

Teeth, 62

Temperament, 48, 65, 104

Terrier Group, 37, 42

The Widow-Maker O'BJ, Ch., 84

Therapy Dogs International, 203

Therapy dogs, 202, 203

Thigh, 87

Tibetan Spaniel, 45

Tibetan Terrier, 45

Topline, 62

Toy Fox Terrier, 44

Toy Group, 37, 44, 45

Toy Manchester Terrier, 44

Toy Poodle, 44

Tracking, 197

Training, 111

Travel, 129-139

    packing, 133, 134

    safety, 131, 132

    temperature, 130, 131

    time, 130, 131

Troymere Believe in Me, Ch., 52

Tumors, 92

Twelve to eighteen month class, 144, 155

Type, 172–178

U

United Kennel Club, 18, 19

United States Dog Agility Association, 193

Upper arms, 63

V

Variety Groups, 36, 37

Veteran classes, 150

Veterinarian, 88-91, 114

Viszla, 38

W

Water, 95

Weguson, Bea, 99

Weimaraner, 38

Welsh Springer Spaniel, 38

Welsh Terrier, 42, 98

West Highland White Terrier, 42, 98

Westminster Kennel Club, 39, 127, 149, 180

Whippet, 40, 52, 53

Wire Fox Terrier, 42, 43, 98

Wirehaired Pointing Griffon, 38

Withers, 86

Wolfpit Cairn Terriers, 100, 101

Working Group, 37, 41

Y

Yorkshire Terrier, 44, 98

Photo Credits

Larry Allen: p. 191, bottom.

Andrews Photo: p. 84.

Ashbey Photos: p. 33; p.39; p. 43; p. 149.

Backstage Photo: p. 79.

Richard Beauchamp: p. 52, bottom; p. 85.

Bergman Photo: p.16, top.

Booth Photo: p.115.

Paulette Braun: p. 108, bottom; p. 201, bottom.

Burwell Photo: p. 53, top right.

Geoff Corrish: p. 51.

Courtesy of the Golden Retriever Club of America: p. 59.

Courtesy of the United Kennel Club: p. 19, top.

Tara Darling: p. 197.

Glenbrook Photo: p.126.

Norma Hamilton: p. 173.

Halfyard Photo: p. 174.

William Holt: p. 53, top left.

Ludwig Photo: p. 155; p. 203.

Lydia Coleman Hutchinson: p.100.

Kalstone Photo: p.116.

Kit Rodwell: p. 179.

Missy Photo: p.123.

Robert Pearcy: p. 198.

Peet Oosthuizen: p. 52, top.

Pegini Photo: p.122.

Photos Today: p. 167.

Roberts Photo: p. 23.

Sabella and Kalstone: p. 163.

Pauline Schultz: p. 187.

Judith Strom: p. 46; p. 190, bottom; p. 191, top; p. 194, bottom; p. 199.

Wayne Cott Photo: p. 185.

All other photos by Isabelle Francais.

Cartoons by Michael Pifer.